Intellectual Leadership in Higher Education

What is 'intellectual leadership' and how might this concept be better understood in the modern university?

Drawing on research into the role of full or chair professors, this book argues that it is important to define and reclaim intellectual leadership as a counter-weight to the prevailing managerial culture of higher education. It contends that professors have been converted into narrowly defined knowledge entrepreneurs and often feel excluded or marginalized as leaders by their own universities. To fulfil their role, professors need to balance the privileges of academic freedom with the responsibilities of academic duty. They exercise their academic freedom as critics and advocates but they also need to be mentors, guardians, enablers and ambassadors. Four orientations to intellectual leadership are identified: *knowledge producer, academic citizen, boundary transgressor* and *public intellectual.* These orientations are illustrated by reference to the careers of professors and show how intellectual leadership can be better understood as a transformational activity. This book tackles the question of what intellectual leadership actually is and analyses the questions most frequently associated with the role of senior academics, including:

- How can intellectual leadership be distinguished from other forms of leadership and management?
- How can professors balance their responsibilities both within and beyond the university?
- How can universities make better use of the expertise of professors as leaders?

It concludes with recommendations for senior institutional managers on how to make more effective use of the expertise and leadership potential of the senior professoriate.

Bruce Macfarlane is Associate Professor for Higher Education at the University of Hong Kong, Hong Kong.

Intellectual Leadership in Higher Education

Renewing the role of the university professor

Bruce Macfarlane

Routledge
Taylor & Francis Group

LONDON AND NEW YORK

First published 2012
by Routledge
2 Park Square, Milton Park, Abingdon, Oxon OX14 4RN together with the
  Society for Research into Higher Education (SRHE)
73 Collier Street
London N1 9BE
UK

Simultaneously published in the USA and Canada
by Routledge
711 Third Avenue, New York, NY 10017 together with the Society for
  Research into Higher Education (SRHE)
73 Collier Street
London N1 9BE
UK

Routledge is an imprint of the Taylor & Francis Group, an informa business

British Library Cataloguing in Publication Data
A catalogue record for this book is available from the British Library

Library of Congress Cataloging in Publication Data
Macfarlane, Bruce, 1961-
Intellectual leadership in higher education : renewing the role of the university
professor / Bruce Macfarlane.
p. cm. -- (Research into higher education)
1. College teachers--Professional relationships. 2. Educational leadership.
I. Title.
LB1778.M24 2012
378.1'2--dc23
2011036752

ISBN: 978-0-415-56081-8 (hbk)
ISBN: 978-0-415-56082-5 (pbk)
ISBN: 978-0-203-81749-0 (ebk)

Typeset in Galliard
by Taylor & Francis Books

For Rachel

Contents

PART 4
Reengagement   **105**

Illustrations

Boxes

Figure

Tables

Series editors' introduction

This series, co-published by the Society for Research into Higher Education and Routledge/Taylor & Francis, aims to provide, in an accessible manner, cutting-edge scholarly thinking and inquiry that reflects the rapidly changing world of higher education, examined in a global context.

Encompassing topics of wide international relevance, the series includes every aspect of the international higher education research agenda, from strategic policy formulation and impact to pragmatic advice on best practice in the field. Each book in the series aims to meet at least one of the principle aims of the Society: to advance knowledge; to enhance practice; to inform policy.

Bruce Macfarlane's Intellectual Leadership in Higher Education constitutes an exemplary start of the series as it addresses a key topic in contemporary higher education. The book contains a sophisticated analysis of the key concepts and is a scholarly contribution with clear imperatives for practice. Although based partly on interviews with UK-based professors, the findings are relevant much more broadly.

Lynn McAlpine
Jeroen Huisman

Foreword

Bruce Macfarlane has done the academic community a number of admirable services through his sequence of books on what constitutes sound ethical practice. This volume presses his careful analysis of academic roles further and deeper. What is special about being a university professor? What should we expect of ourselves, and what are others entitled to expect of us?

'Intellectual leadership' looks like a good answer, but as Macfarlane carefully sets out, it doesn't necessarily come with the title or the (enhanced or not) paycheque.

One of the major faults of the modern academy is its loss of respect for our sacred words (like 'excellence'). Another is the relentless rise of self-ascription, at an individual as well as an institutional level. Like all other forms of leadership, genuine intellectual leadership has to be earned, not asserted. Empty institutional claims about 'world-classness' are not that far away from some individuals' aggressive self-promotion as 'public intellectuals' or 'thought leaders'.

It's a commonly recognised trait of great sportsmen and women as well as musicians that those who can really 'do it' don't have to tell you. There's a humility, and an associated generosity of spirit, about the unquestionably top performers. The same can be true of some leaders in academic fields, although aspects of our internal culture militate against these traits. Consider the hyperbole to which senior academics can resort when talking about things they don't really understand: as Macfarlane generously acknowledges, it's one of my most robust 'laws' of academic life that individuals gain in confidence the further they are away from their true field of expertise. Among higher education institutional leaders the right mixture is rare, although I have observed it: the late Lord Eric Ashby had both of these key qualities, and was extraordinarily effective.

So, to follow the line of argument that I can acknowledge or grant intellectual leadership (the reciprocal of which is that I'm not prepared to have it thrust upon me), where do I find it? For me it is at least as much outside as within the academy. And the discovery is very much correlated with my personal (including private) interests.

The people who 'do it' for me include: great pianists (and thinkers about their art and what it means more broadly) like Alfred Brendel and Mitsuko Uchida; novelists, including from the popular end of the street, like John Le Carré (an extraordinary gazetteer of our evolving socio-political situation) or Sue Thompson (whose structured observations of our culture are for me as powerful as those of George Orwell); and (in my own academic field) historians of ideas like Richard Sennett, Quentin Skinner and Bruce Kuklick.

The real virtue of Macfarlane's *Intellectual Leadership in Higher Education* is its further demonstration, on both theoretical and empirical levels, of gaps between what we say and what we do: who we think we are, and how we appear to others. Renewing the role of the professoriate is going to require precisely the sort of disciplined self-reflection set out in this useful book.

David Watson
Green Templeton College, Oxford
2 July 2011

Acknowledgements

I am indebted to a number of people. First, I would like to thank David Watson for writing the Foreword. His ideas along with those of other colleagues interested in the concept of intellectual leadership, such as Paul Blackmore, have contributed to my own thinking in grappling with this topic over the last few years. My thanks also go to Jingjing Zhang for helping me with elements of the Chinese context of higher education and Roy Chan for the analysis of academic obituaries and proofreading.

The book would not have been possible without the cooperation of university professors who were kind enough to either complete my questionnaire and/or agree to be interviewed by me. I have further benefited from opportunities to present my ideas on intellectual leadership at various conferences and seminars. The feedback from participants on these occasions is always helpful and has helped me to sharpen and refine my analysis.

I would like to record my thanks to Joelle Fanghanel, Jon Nixon and Roger Ottewill who gave me valuable feedback on a draft of the manuscript and made many useful suggestions for improvement.

The book draws on some of my recent research into the work and activities of professors, some of which was funded by the UK Leadership Foundation, including the following articles:

Macfarlane, B. (2011) The morphing of academic practice: unbundling and the para-academic, *Higher Education Quarterly*, 65:1, pp. 59–73.

Macfarlane, B. (2011) Professors as intellectual leaders: formation, identity and role, *Studies in Higher Education*, 36:1, 57–73.

Finally, but most importantly, this book is dedicated to Rachel Chong. I have loved her since we first met 32 years ago. Madly, deeply, completely. Fools give you reasons. Wise men never try.

Part 1

Leadership and intellectuals

Chapter 1

Introduction

The leadership crisis

A curious omission

There are lots of books and articles about intellectuals and many others that focus on the meaning of leadership. However, to my knowledge, there are very few that have tried to understand how these terms may be conjoined in a meaningful way. Although intellectual leadership sounds like a nice phrase, it tends to be used as an appeal or an assertion with limited explanation as to what it actually implies in practice. So, what exactly is intellectual leadership? This book sets out to answer this question and others associated with the role of senior academics as intellectual leaders.

My attempt to tackle this subject will draw mainly on my research into the role of university professors, some of which is previously reported elsewhere (Macfarlane, 2011a). By a 'university professor' I do not mean everyone holding a substantive role as an academic. I am using the word professor in the more selective sense of those who hold a full professorial title or endowed Chair at a university or other higher education institution. They are essentially the senior faculty members with either the formal or informal responsibility to lead others. Often this expectation is implied rather than stated specifically in a professor's contract of employment.

It seems strange that there are so few references to professors and intellectual leadership in books about higher education. This does not seem like an odd omission just to me. As others have commented, the professoriate is curiously missing from the scholarly work on academic management and there is no educational theory of leadership linked to the work of professors (Rayner *et al.*, 2010, p. 618). Hence, this is a book about the concept of intellectual leadership linked to gaining a greater understanding of the role of university professors.

Who is an 'intellectual leader'?

Clearly, university professors are not the only ones who might lay claim to being intellectual leaders. The professorial title alone is just that, a title. Indeed, in the increasingly competitive and individualist world of global higher education being a professor may be seen as little more than a career grade; an affirmation of status and prestige rather than a position carrying additional responsibilities. Professors are, of course, not the only ones who lead. Other academics can also be influential figures but may not, for whatever reason, have been promoted to a full Chair. Moreover, academics are just one, perhaps increasingly marginalized, group of cultural producers in modern society. Others with intellectual influence include journalists, lawyers, government advisors, media commentators and, indeed, anyone prepared to adopt a critical and independent stance and give voice to their analysis of the world through some form of oral or written publication. In 2005 (and again in 2008), *Foreign Policy* magazine teamed up with *Prospect* to produce a poll of the world's top 100 intellectuals (Prospect, 2005). The poll defined an intellectual as someone who has shown distinction in their own field along with the ability to communicate ideas and influence debate outside of it. Many of those listed were from outside academe including religious leaders, politicians and journalists. However, the vast majority still had some former or current connection with academic life.

While the term intellectual tends to be used by people by exception, it is broad-ranging in other ways. Intellectuals may come from many parts of society and are not necessarily holders of high public office or those with conventional academic qualifications. Indeed, a number of writers have argued that the modern academic, increasingly corralled into fragmented sub-disciplines and subject to the conformist pressures of professionalization, is anything but intellectual in orientation (Fuller, 2005). The growth of the internet means that blogging, podcasts and social networking are avenues by which anyone can establish themselves as an authority on a subject and potentially gain a following. The opportunity to be influential may not be open to all but helps to give a voice to many more. In this way the internet has a democratizing effect as a communication tool. Alert academics are also realizing the potential of technology to reach a wider and more global audience for their ideas.

Despite the opportunity for more to engage in public debate, the university, even in its modern form, is an environment from which we might still expect many intellectuals to emerge (Roberts, 2007). Pierre Bourdieu, Germaine Greer and Noam Chomsky, for example, all forged their careers in academia before reaching wider attention as public intellectuals. Furthermore, the (full) professorial title does single out an individual academic as possessing a serious scholarly reputation at the very least. Professors are senior figures within universities who have historically played an influential role in the life of the university, and wider society. It is for this reason that it seems entirely appropriate to mainly focus my attention on this group of individuals. What is the role of the modern university professor? How can their activities and commitments help us to better understand what intellectual leadership means? How can intellectual leadership be reasserted or reestablished? Seeking an answer to these and other questions related to the meaning of intellectual leadership will form the core purpose of this book.

Intellectual leadership is an expression frequently invoked in books, articles and speeches but surprisingly few manage to say much about what it means. It is, obviously, 'a good thing' but is too often used as little more than an appealing mantra or hurrah phrase. Worse, intellectual leadership can be used as a slightly pompous or patronizing entreaty to, for example, raise the 'tone' of debate or develop a more 'cultured' society. This harks back to an elitist idea of culture as promoted by the poet and cultural commentator Matthew Arnold in the nineteenth century (Arnold, 1869).

There have been isolated attempts to define what intellectual leadership means in connection with higher education. J. Patrick Conroy's book, *Intellectual Leadership in Education* (Conroy, 2000), for example, offers a guide to the history of Western intellectual traditions rather than an exploration of academic leadership. A recent and more relevant example to my project is a study of the work of deans of education (Wepner *et al.*, 2008). This identified a conceptual model consisting of four leadership dimensions: intellectual, emotional, social and moral. Of the four dimensions, the intellectual was the most frequently used by the deans of education who were the subject of the study. According to this study, the intellectual dimension comprised themes including tolerating ambiguity, the ability to see reality as complex and contradictory, recognizing individual differences, defining problems, making decisions and seeking information (Wepner *et al.*, 2008).

This list of qualities or traits associated with intellectual leadership is indicative of what I would call educated uncertainty rather than certainty. The tolerance of ambiguity demands an ability to understand that reality is a contested and complex concept. While 'making decisions' is included in the list, much of the emphasis is on being able to conceptualize and empathize. It is, in other words, far removed from the often macho image of the 'great leader'. What is notable is that few of these qualities are straightforward or even teachable skills. This is indicative of the familiar assertion that while a leader can be taught certain managerial or technical skills, such as budgeting or recruitment procedures, a manager cannot be taught to lead. The presumption here is that a leader is 'born' rather than 'made'. While this list of qualities pertaining to intellectual leadership is helpful, it does not have anything special to say about leadership in an academic context, with which I am concerned. The qualities identified might equally be found in some business leaders or politicians. My aim is to define intellectual leadership in a way that is more relevant to an academic context as opposed to any context.

Intellectual leadership is clearly about more than a set of functions that any educated individual can be trained to perform. Yet this does not exclude the idea that people can become better leaders through acquiring new skills. I will argue that while someone may have the credentials to be an intellectual leader, partly through the power of their intellect and prior academic achievements, this in itself is not enough. Leadership further demands a care and a concern for others. As such, there are dispositions and skills associated with academic duty that an intellectual leader also needs (see Chapter 8).

Leadership and management

It is also important to say what this book is not about. It is not a book about management in the sense in which this word is commonly used. What I mean by this is that the word management tends to be largely associated with *formal* roles, where the role holder is often called a manager and has a job description that details responsibilities linked to this expectation. Research studies about leadership in higher education tend to be dominated by this focus (Middlehurst, 2008). In practice, in a higher education context, academic leadership is highly *distributed* (Bolden *et al.*, 2008). In other words, it can be found anywhere in an organization and much of it is social, tacit and situated in nature. There are rows of books about what it means to be a university or college president and a growing literature about being a head of department (e.g. Knight and Trowler, 2001) or dean (e.g. Bright and Richards, 2001; Harman, 2002) but very little about the *informal* leadership offered by the professoriate and other academics. This is a critical point.

But where can we start? Even the leadership literature has comparatively little specific to say about intellectual leadership, and it is rarely mentioned even in books that assemble an encyclopaedia of concepts (e.g. Marturano and Gosling, 2008). There is, however, a possible link between intellectual leadership and the concept of transformational leadership. This latter concept is associated with a number of characteristics including charisma, a strong ability to inspire others, stimulating others intellectually and giving people personal attention, or what is described as 'individualized consideration' in the leadership jargon (Burns, 1978; Yukl, 2002). These characteristics have been summarized as visioning, challenging, enabling, modelling and encouraging (Kouzes and Posner, 1993). These are things one might also expect to find in an intellectual leader including, hopefully, university professors. Beyond this, I believe that intellectual leadership is further connected to someone being seen to have moral power or authority.

Transformational leadership is normally contrasted with its less glamorous counterpart, transactional leadership. This depends for authority on followers' acceptance of hierarchy and the deployment of rewards and penalties. Transactional leadership is essentially an economic exchange based on self-interest, whilst transformational leadership is about mutuality of interest. It depends on more than just carrots and sticks to punish and motivate people in other words. Being a transformational leader involves the ability to inspire others and bring about some form of change. In the same way, one might expect academics who are leaders in their field to help to bring about a paradigmatic transformation in the way that knowledge about the world is understood (McGee Banks, 1995). Hence, transformational leadership is possibly the closest cousin to intellectual leadership and might reasonably be applied to the role of professors as leaders (Hogg, 2007).

In exploring further what leadership means in the context of academic life it is useful to draw on Martin Trow's identification of four dimensions: symbolic, political, managerial and academic (Trow, 2010a). Even though these four dimensions are based on the presumption that the leader is a college or university president or vice chancellor, they provide a means of understanding different elements of what it means to be any kind of leader in a higher education context. Symbolic leadership is the way in which someone can come to represent a particular organization, movement or project. This might not involve their active participation in the day-to-day affairs of leadership but their personality or reputation somehow embodies it. Aung San Suu Kyi became an internationally recognized symbol of the political opposition in Burma whilst kept under house arrest by the military regime there for many years. During the time in which she was detained a series of international honours and awards, including the Nobel Peace Prize, were bestowed on her. The Nobel Peace Prize is perhaps the most well-known international honour, and the publicity generated by the award can have a powerful effect in further bolstering the symbolic leadership of a recipient. In 2010 the Chinese human rights campaigner Liu Xiaobo was the recipient, having been sentenced to 11 years in prison in 2009. Universities often have symbolic heads who mainly undertake ceremonial functions and whose image or fame provides a marketing value. Chancellors of English universities perform this role, for example.

Trow defines political leadership as the ability to deal with the conflicting demands and pressures of different constituencies both within and external to the university. This demands adroitness, persuasion and diplomatic skills in keeping a variety of parties or stakeholders happy whilst still being able to make effective decisions. Managerial leadership, on the other hand, involves financial and budgetary skills, effective control over human and physical resources, and planning for the future. Finally, academic management involves other qualities such as the ability to spot, recruit and give appropriate support to talented individuals in relation to teaching and research. New managerialism (see Chapter 3) has tended to elevate the importance of leadership by managers at the expense of academics. I will argue that it is important to rebalance things a little by reevaluating the role of professors as leaders.

One of the problems with the phrase academic leadership (or academic management) is whether it means the leadership *of* academics or leadership *by* academics. It can, of course, refer to both, but often there is some ambiguity as to whether it implies that academics are managing or leading themselves or being led by a professional manager. When I refer to intellectual leadership I am limiting my discussion mainly to the ways in which professors as senior members of the academic profession are performing as leaders often in an informal sense. What I mean by informal is that they are untitled leaders unlike deans or vice chancellors but are nonetheless providing a focal point and enacting behaviours that are central to leadership.

Part of my purpose is to offer some ideas about how the role of professors as leaders might be better understood in response to the dearth of literature on the subject. Another part of the argument of this book is that senior academics have a responsibility to lead and to 'get their hands dirty' as leaders rather than standing aloof. The notion that intellectuals should not sully their hands with the responsibilities of leadership is a conceit that deserves to be challenged. As I will argue, intellectual leadership is about duty as well as freedom. However, it is not only incumbent on intellectuals to get involved in leadership. It is also important for universities to recognize that leaders will not be followed (or perhaps even respected) without intellectual credibility or authority. In other words, successful university leadership depends as much upon *who* you are as on what someone may be able to offer in terms of managerial and other technical skills. Unless someone first possesses an academic and intellectual reputation for their scholarly achievements it is less likely that faculty members will be prepared to follow that person and respect their authority as a formally designated leader.

Research shows that the best university leaders of research-based institutions are scholars rather than administrators (Goodall, 2009). According to this analysis, institutional performance is improved when top scholars are put in charge of universities. This is attributed to the fact that human nature leads people to prioritize things that they are most interested in. For university academics the priority is research. Hence, when you place a researcher in charge of a university they focus on the university's research performance. This has become the way that elite institutions distinguish themselves from competitors. Other professionals, such as lawyers or medical doctors, are accustomed to being led by their peers. Why should academics be any different?

The crisis of confidence

In some ways the very idea of leadership by professionals is in crisis. A view has taken hold that professionals, especially those working in the public services, cannot be trusted to lead themselves. Instead, the view of recent governments seems to have been that leadership responsibilities need to be hived off to professional managers in the health service, in doctor's practices and in universities. But what have been the consequences of this thinking? One has been that management roles have lost respect as a result of their professionalization and separation from those undertaking the main professional role in the organization, be they a doctor, a police officer, a teacher or a university academic. This is now acting as a barrier in getting the best academics to take on leadership and management roles. Why would anyone want to undertake a role that garners so little respect? It is not an exaggeration, I believe, to call this a leadership crisis.

In investigating what it means to be an intellectual leader in higher education I have drawn on a variety of primary and secondary sources of evidence. The book is partly based on research conducted for a project funded by the UK Leadership foundation for higher education in 2008 and 2009. This included interviews with university professors from a range of disciplines. It also draws on a larger survey of 233 mainly UK-based professors asked to comment on how they perceived their role as professors and leaders. Finally, the book relies on a collection of obituaries about leading academics as a means of illustrating the concept of intellectual leadership by reference to a wider group of influential academics (see Chapter 9).

Conclusion

In summary, I believe it is an important time to re-evaluate what we mean by intellectual leadership for a number of reasons. First, the university's role in society is being increasingly challenged as a transmitter, preserver and creator of knowledge. The internet search engine Google is arguably now a more powerful transmitter of knowledge than the university. This does not mean that universities do not have a critical role as knowledge producers, but it does imply that they need to refocus their energies on creativity and criticality as intellectual enterprises. Second, university leadership and management is still equated almost exclusively with the role and responsibilities of those occupying formal management roles such as heads of department, deans, vice presidents and pro vice chancellors, presidents and vice chancellors. Yet this characterization seems out of step with the emphasis in the contemporary literature in thinking about leadership as both informal and distributed. Finally, as participation in higher education has grown on a global basis, there has been a considerable increase of academic faculty as new universities have been formed and old ones expanded.

In this context, there is now a much larger professoriate. In the UK, over 17,000 members of faculty hold a full professorial title (HESA, 2009). What is the role of these senior members of the academic profession? What expectations do universities have of them and how do they see their own role? I will also reflect on how, having better understood what professors are for, institutions might make better use of their expertise.

In this first part of the book, I will outline what I see as the 'retreat' of the modern professoriate. This will examine how conventional forms of academic and intellectual leadership have been displaced by a managerial culture. It is also connected with the changing nature of academic life and the way in which individualized achievement as a researcher has come to define the role of the modern professor undermining a broader commitment to service and leadership.

In Part 2, I will outline how intellectual leadership is being undermined at both the individual level and through the ways in which universities are corporatizing the research agenda. Part 3 of the book is based on my empirical research into the role of professors as leaders, and as such considers the process for becoming a professor and how professors see their own role. Here, I am drawing on what I consider to be an important distinction between *becoming* a professor and what *being* one means in practice. I will further identify two freedoms central to intellectual leadership – being a critic and an advocate – and four duties – being a mentor, a guardian of standards, an enabler of networking and resources for others, and an ambassador for the institution or discipline.

In the final section (Part 4) I will suggest ways in which intellectual leadership may be reclaimed. At the individual level, I will present a model of intellectual leadership with four possible orientations for professors drawing on academic obituaries (see Chapter 9). I will argue that universities also need to display a commitment to intellectual leadership by embracing their historic role as a critical conscience and using a moral compass, particularly when developing relationships with other higher education providers on an international basis (Chapter 10). The final chapter will offer a series of recommendations aimed at university senior managers, suggesting how the professoriate might be reengaged and better developed for an intellectual leadership role.

In summary, I will argue that:

- professors need to balance the privileges of academic freedom with the responsibilities of academic duty;
- intellectual leadership in higher education may be understood in terms of four principal orientations: knowledge producer, academic citizen, boundary transgressor and public intellectual;
- universities should reconnect with and uphold their own values as a critical conscience of society in offering intellectual leadership; and
- universities need to (re)define the role of professors and their expectations of them more clearly and utilize their skills as locals as well as cosmopolitans.

I hope the ideas that I present in this book will provide a basis for a reevaluation of the role of professors in higher education as intellectual leaders rather than the more narrowly constructed debate, as I see it, which divides university academic from management roles. This dichotomy, like many others, is essentially erroneous and fails to capture the complexity of a more nuanced situation. Intellectual leadership is a form of leadership that is central to the purpose of the university, and this book will seek to explore both its meaning and how it can be reinvigorated.

Chapter 2

Beyond the caricature

Introduction

Intellectual leadership is a powerful phrase. It projects seriousness and authority, combining the notion of a leader who is also an intelligent thinker or scholar. It is an ideal like democratic government or unspoilt beauty. Many of the great social and political figures of the past – Mahatma Ghandi, Martin Luther King, Abraham Lincoln, Nelson Mandela or Emmeline Pankhurst to name but a few – might popularly be considered intellectual leaders. They combined charisma and moral strength with ideas and a desire to change society on the basis of strongly held principles. All these individuals were fired by ideas and ideals and were, critically, able to inspire, lead and, ultimately, change or reshape the attitudes of others. Their leadership carried an authority and a moral persuasiveness rather than one based on any coercion or 'muscle'. Intellectual leaders mobilize others through inspiration rather than fear.

Figures from the literary world have also been influential in raising awareness of social and political issues through their novels. In books such as *Oliver Twist*, for example, the British novelist Charles Dickens exposed the injustices of Victorian society. In response to the corruption of communism under Stalin, George Orwell produced the classic satire *Animal Farm*. Other lesser known figures today were influential in their lifetime in bringing about political change, such as Caroline Norton, a campaigner for women's rights in the nineteenth century, who produced a satirical novel entitled *The Wife*. Occasionally musicians can prove inspirational figures too. The lyrics of Argentinian folk singer Facundo Cabral helped to galvanize opposition to South American military dictatorships in the 1970s. Beyond the literary and music worlds, some business leaders, such as Anita Roddick, may be thought of as offering forms of intellectual leadership. She demonstrated that a passion for environmentalism and social justice could be incorporated into a successful business model. The theme of social responsibility also underpins the achievements of Muhammad Yunus, a Bangladeshi economist, widely regarded as the founding father of micro-financing. Yunus' Grameen Bank loans relatively small amounts of money to poor entrepreneurs as a means of lifting people out of poverty.

Hence, individuals offering intellectual leadership come from many fields of endeavour, including politics and religion, the arts, and business and commerce. They can be found as much beyond the university as within it. This chapter will consider how academics working in universities might fit into this broader picture. It will also explore the origins, assumptions and multiple meanings of 'intellectual' and consider the challenge of defining intellectual leadership.

A paradox

Intellectual leadership is a problematic term. It might even be considered a contradiction in terms. The popular impression is that it is one thing to be an intellectual and quite another to be an effective leader. We are all familiar with the caricature of the intellectual. Such people are highly intelligent but often so engrossed with their own thoughts that they can appear eccentric and unable to cope with the more mundane side of life. This 'other worldliness' can make intellectuals seem self-absorbed or, perhaps, even selfish individuals. Intellectuals may be clever but they can also, in more negative ways, be characterized as unworldly. They can cope with conceptual complexity but not with the simpler things in life. According to the American politician Spiro Agnew, an intellectual is a man who doesn't know how to park a bike. Neither are intellectuals seen as particularly well organized, dependable or even responsible toward others; all qualities that one might expect of a good leader. Almost by definition, as creative and free thinkers, intellectuals are individualistic. They are not seen as sufficiently responsible to be put in charge of collective activities. It is best to leave them alone to do what they excel at – to have great thoughts and come up with new ideas. They are iconoclasts rather than joiners; too autonomous to be roped into any real responsibilities. The feeling here is that putting intellectuals in charge of things is asking for trouble, as while they may be clever they can also be awkward and irresponsible mavericks.

The British politician Michael Foot, who died in 2010 at the age of 96, was perhaps a good example of the commonsense theory that intellectuals do not make effective leaders. Foot was probably best known as a Labour party politician, a long-serving member of the British Parliament who later became a cabinet minister, and for three years in the early 1980s the leader of the opposition. Foot was a committed socialist who also enjoyed a successful career as a political journalist and was the author of a large number of books and articles about politics, including a biography of his hero, and fellow Labour Party politician, Aneurin Bevan. Foot became leader of the Labour Party quite late in his career at a time when the Conservative Party was in the ascendancy. He led it into the 1983 general election with a highly radical party political manifesto that promised, amongst other things, unilateral nuclear disarmament and the abolition of the House of Lords, the hereditary-based upper chamber of the UK Parliament. The manifesto was caustically described by one of Foot's Labour party colleagues, Gerald Kaufman, as 'the longest suicide note in history' (Kavanagh, 2000, p. 4). Labour subsequently suffered one of its worst electoral defeats. While a fervent and, at times, amusing speaker, Foot was also seen as ill-suited to the slick new age of television politics. His choice of an insufficiently formal overcoat at a Remembrance Day ceremony is an oft-quoted incident that illustrated his unwillingness to adjust his appearance to create a media-friendly image.

Foot also lacked something that all leaders need: luck or good fortune. Shortly after becoming Labour leader, serious internal division occurred when four senior party figures formed a breakaway party, which quickly picked up considerable public support. Then, in 1982, the defeat of Argentina by Britain in the Falklands conflict boosted the popularity of the incumbent Conservative government. Foot's defeat at the 1983 general election followed. Hence, although Michael Foot was a much-admired 'conviction' politician, he is not regarded as someone who offered a successful model of leadership. He remained a radical and an intellectual long after his retirement from active politics, committed to campaigning for nuclear disarmament until the very end of his life.

The example of Michael Foot might appear to confirm the common impression that intellectual leadership is a contradiction in terms but then, perhaps, it merely illustrates that not all intellectuals necessarily make good, or maybe just lucky, political leaders. Foot offered a leadership in respect of ideas connected with radical socialism and was possibly most successful in this role as a campaigning left-wing politician and journalist. Here, he was an influential intellectual leader in terms of his contributions to the discussion and analysis of socialism. Foot was held in high regard by figures across the political spectrum partly because he was not seen as someone prepared to compromise his beliefs for the sake of political expediency.

While Foot had very strong academic and intellectual credentials, strangely, other political leaders have been lauded for *not* possessing any intellectual credentials. A lack of academic credentials is sometimes made into a virtue that 'qualifies' them to better understand the problems facing the populace. Former US President George W. Bush was hailed for his lack of cerebration (Mead, 2010). Directly the opposite observation was made about Barack Obama, who holds a number of degrees. Critics expressed their fears that 'pointy-headed intellectuals' are ill-suited to govern (quoted in Mead, 2010). The same inverted snobbery can be found among some individuals in the world of commerce and entrepreneurship, where it is conventional to claim that being a student of the so-called 'university of life' is a superior education for the cut and thrust of business life. But, despite this popular imagery, there are examples of intellectuals who have, arguably, made successful political leaders, such as Thomas Jefferson and well-educated business leaders. Intellectual leadership may be a paradox but it is not necessarily an oxymoron.

A conceit?

Another accusation laid at the door of the intellectual is that they are simply egocentric individuals. Claiming to be, or having aspirations to become, 'an intellectual' is in itself sometimes regarded in negative terms. It might appear self-important implying that one is mentally superior to others. This gives rise to the idea that intellectuals are snobs. They think they are better than everyone else and want to self-consciously stand apart. They can appear cold, unapproachable and remote, making them a possible target of abuse and blame. One of the goals of the cultural revolution in China during the 1960s and 1970s was to eliminate class distinctions between intellectuals, workers and peasants as part of so-called 'class levelling'.

Another way of characterizing intellectuals is that they are essentially boorish figures of fun, guilty of taking themselves too seriously. From an English cultural perspective there is said to be a taboo on earnestness (Fox, 2004) or, as Georges Mikes put it more simply, 'in England it is bad manners to be clever' (Mikes, 1946, p. 36). Claiming to be an intellectual or to offer intellectual leadership can be regarded as little more than a conceit. Paul Johnson's book *Intellectuals* (1988) contains sketches of influential figures from the history of politics, literature and philosophy, including Rousseau, Marx, Tolstoy and Sartre. The French philosopher Jean-Jacques Rousseau is portrayed as a vain individual with 'a high opinion of himself' (p. 6) who 'felt too superior to hate' (p. 10). The poet Shelley was a 'sublime egoist' (p. 36), the political theorist Karl Marx 'resented the smallest criticism' (p. 73) while 'creative selfishness' (p. 96) lay at the heart of playwright Henrik Ibsen's personal doctrine. These represent just a few of dozens of references to the egocentricity and character flaws of this highly influential selection of intellectuals. While all of them were hugely talented individuals, conceited self-regard appears to be a frequently occurring personal characteristic.

The caricature of the intellectual sketched above appears to have more than a germ of truth in it, yet there are other dimensions to consider in understanding who intellectuals are. Most serious writing about the identity of intellectuals portrays them as 'outsiders' rather than as 'insiders' (Said, 1994). They are individuals who stand outside of, or perhaps even aloof from, the organization, profession or nation-state. They are freewheeling, rebellious, sceptical critics rather than loyal employees or followers. They retain their critical gaze through remaining outside of the established order and are often exiles in both a literal and metaphorical sense. Much of the language used to characterize the intellectual is resonant of this stance. According to Bourdieu (1989) an intellectual is a bi-dimensional being; someone who belongs to an autonomous field of intellectual study (such as an academic or a scientist) and who uses their authority and competence as an expert to undertake a political action that is 'carried out outside the intellectual field proper' (p. 656). In many ways intellectuals see themselves as advocates speaking on behalf of the disenfranchised; the representative of those that are marginalized in society. As I will argue later in the book, this advocacy role is one of several qualities of an intellectual leader (see Chapter 7).

Hence, the intellectual is someone who feels impelled to campaign and comment about topics of public interest that are not necessarily part of their formal knowledge base. Put in a less censorious way, they are interested in offering a view outside their immediate specialism, as, say, a historian or bioscientist. This is why intellectuals can sometimes be referred to as 'amateurs' rather than 'professionals' (Said, 1994). Here, the term is used in a positive sense since intellectuals are not representing the view of an established 'insider' or someone with an 'expert', and perhaps narrowly conventional, opinion. As a result intellectuals often challenge the status quo or the establishment perspective.

However, the term amateur is also often used in a more critical, censorious way. One of Watson's (2009) tongue-in-cheek laws of academic life is that individuals gain in confidence the further they are away from their true field of expertise. This acerbic comment elegantly presents the most common criticism of those who might self-ascribe the status of public intellectual. Academics who want to venture beyond the cognitive borderland of their discipline also risk accusations of over-simplification or being publicity seekers (Brock, 1996). Yet individuals who want to influence attitudes in society are often drawn into contestation beyond their immediate academic specialism. Richard Dawkins, an academic biologist, is probably better known as an atheist and critic of religion (see Chapter 7). Figures from other walks of life, including celebrities, can take on advocacy roles outside of their professional specialism. Film actor Richard Gere, for example, is an active campaigner for human rights in Tibet.

There will be those who regard the contributions of such individuals beyond their immediate professional specialism as a positive indicator of their commitment to making a better society or standing up for the disenfranchised or oppressed. But equally there are those who see their activities in more critical terms, as narcissistic and self-publicizing. This was a charge laid at the door of radical intellectuals in the 1960s such as Norman Mailer (Johnson, 1988). While the desire to contribute to public debate can be seen as a responsibility for those working in universities and research institutes, it also risks censor as an abuse of power or image-conscious behaviour, in the same way as pop stars or film actors can be mocked for offering opinions on political issues. Beyond concerns about a lack of personal modesty, Johnson (1988) argues that there is a more fundamental danger in allowing intellectuals to acquire the benefits of a public platform. He contends that intellectuals have contributed to experiments in 'social engineering' that have led directly to the death of millions of innocent people. Their utopianism, as Johnson sees it, represents a threat to society by putting ideas before the welfare of people. This is the same, somewhat curious, line of argument by which the degree-less George W. Bush was trumpeted as less of a danger to the world than the degree-holding Barack Obama during the 2008 US presidential campaign.

Despite such criticisms, intellectuals have always been associated with campaigning on social and political issues. This may be traced back to the Dreyfus affair in France long acknowledged to be the birth of the idea of the intellectual as we might understand it today (Drake, 2005). Alfred Dreyfus was an Alsatian Jew who held the rank of Captain in the French army. In 1894 he was convicted of treason for allegedly sending military secrets to the German Embassy in Paris.

Later it became apparent that his conviction was based on false evidence and, through the campaigning of the novelist Emile Zola and other writers and scientists, Dreyfus was eventually exonerated and reinstated in the French army. However, the affair had a profound impact on French society, dividing opinion starkly between those that supported Dreyfus (the 'Dreyfusards') and anti-semitic campaigners who regarded him as a traitor (the 'anti-Dreyfusards'). Subsequently, intellectuals in France and elsewhere became known for their opposition to nationalism, anti-semitism, fascism and the power of the church, whilst promoting pacifism and communism. Hence, intellectuals tend to be anti-establishment and are principally associated with 'the left' politically, although there are exceptions of individuals who might be more closely allied with 'the right'. Intellectuals have authority as knowledgeable, autonomous or independent thinkers, rather than powerful role holders. This is normally derived from being separated from the world of politics. Instead, they tend to be mainly drawn from the world of the arts, science and literature (Bourdieu, 1989) and seek to 'speak the truth to power' (Said, 1994, p. xiv). Intellectuals continue to play a more important role in French society, where figures like Bernard-Henri Lévy and Philippe Sollers are influential public commentators and opinion formers, compared with Britain where a more satirical and self-mocking image prevails and fewer intellectual voices are heard as a result.

However, some see the role of the contemporary intellectual as essentially bankrupt and as little more than an opportunistic mouthpiece for whatever the market demands (Gordon, 2010). Here, it is said that the growing market for intellectual ideas, through the expansion of the media and the World Wide Web, has led to the market colonization of intellectuals (Gordon, 2010). This has a number of features including the commodification of intellectual effort via quantitative metrics based on publications, the perceived quality of their scholarly output based on journal rankings, and the number of times others have cited their work (see Chapter 9). Scholars now compete to get into the media rather than maintaining a healthy distance from it. Universities have marketing and corporate communications departments that seek to promote the expertise of their faculty members and promote the image of the institution via media contributions. According to Gordon, some scholars now function more like brand names and are perpetually 'on the market' selling their academic wares. Knowledge itself is now market driven and, hence, intellectuals must respond to the needs of the media rather than shaping debate and performing an educative function. Gordon's argument has much in common with that of Zygmunt Bauman (1987), who has powerfully argued that the role of the intellectual has shifted in postmodern society from that of a legislator of ideas to a diminished interpreter of events.

The leader and the intellectual

In many ways the caricature of an intellectual stands in sharp contrast with that of a leader. This is mainly connected with the way in which leaders are often expected to commit to collective goals and possess strong social skills. Being an iconoclast is about asserting one's individuality rather than trying to respond to the needs of others. However, while leaders may not generally be thought to possess qualities that are necessarily associated with being an intellectual, there is still common ground. In the popular imagination leaders, like intellectuals, are seen as strong, persuasive and charismatic. Sometimes this involves possessing a degree of arrogance that is representative of an assured self-confidence. The English soccer manager Brian Clough was renowned for his arrogance mixed with Northern English humour. He once famously quipped: 'I wouldn't say I was the best manager in the business. But I was in the top one'.

Leaders need to be intelligent and capable. Capability depends on context and includes good judgement and mental alertness, not just intelligence. In other words, leaders are thought to need some combination of academic and practical capacities. One conventional way of thinking about leadership is in terms of traits or characteristics that make a good leader. Traits include responsibility and highlight qualities such as being dependable, well organized and taking the initiative. Leaders are also thought to need strong interpersonal skills that make them cooperative, sociable and sensitive to the views and feelings of others (Stogdill, 1974). Hence, a good leader is normally considered to need strong administrative and interpersonal or social skills, not just a good brain (Boyatzis, 1982). This means an ability not just to communicate with others in a language they can understand but to exercise a range of appropriate emotional responses when dealing with others such as sympathy, empathy and a preparedness to listen. The purpose of discussion for an intellectual though might be more about winning the argument rather than listening and being persuaded of an alternative view or course of action. As Brian Clough once said: 'if I had an argument with a player we would sit down for twenty minutes, talk about it and then decide I was right!' Understanding others takes time and patience and a concern for others. Such selfless social qualities are rarely associated with the intellectual or indeed charismatic leaders.

The representation of the intellectual is as a solitary figure, with clear, even fixed views rather than a more malleable individual able to empathize and colla- borate with others. Intellectuals are not automatically associated with strong interpersonal skills, a sense of communal responsibility or a preparedness to share power or authority. This might partly be because they believe that they are right and do not need to consider the views of others. Intellectuals may not even want followers and can be keen to avoid any form of formal leadership role as an insi- der, preferring to remain on the outside of professional organizations and insti- tutions. The exclusion of intellectuals from leadership roles may be compounded by the notion that insiders, rather than outsiders, are the ones who tend to be more trusted to lead by groups, commercial and professional organizations. Insiders may not be as talented but they are often seen as a safer choice.

But there are also parallels between popular notions of leadership and the car- icature of the intellectual. Most attention has tended to focus on the idea of the heroic or charismatic leader. This concept of leadership is often illustrated through reference to political, religious or military leaders of the past, such as Napoleon, Winston Churchill or Mother Theresa. Characterizing leadership in terms of 'greatness' or 'charisma' means that such a status is seen as something exceptional, rather than commonly attainable. A tiny minority might be considered charismatic or great, otherwise such terms would lose their resonance or force. This implies that leadership is about the possession of an elite quality that, in reality, few can hope to aspire to or be assigned by others. It was not until the latter part of the twentieth century that serious academic interest in leadership picked up and moved beyond the simple notion of the 'great' leader by beginning to understand the importance of process and participation rather than the actions of a single person (Marturano and Gosling, 2008).

Modern leadership theory recognizes the fact that leaders can be found across a broader spectrum of individuals within groups and in a variety of contexts and situations not just at the top. This idea is normally referred to as distributed leadership. Leaders can be found at lots of different levels both within and outside organizations. Distributed leadership is a more inclusive conception that takes account of the role of a wider range of actors. It suggests that it is too simplistic to divide people into leaders or followers. There is a recognition here that many individuals make leadership work, that the sources of leadership influence are much more varied than previously acknowledged and that, in practice, expertise is shared among many people rather than just limited to a tiny cadre of the 'great' or the 'good'.

In parallel with the study of leadership more generally, this understanding has only recently begun to permeate interest in university leadership. Most studies have conventionally focused on the role of formally designated senior managers, such as presidents, vice chancellors, vice presidents and pro-vice chancellors and those with more immediate responsibility for academic units such as deans of faculty and heads of department (e.g. Warner and Palfreyman, 2000; Shattock, 2003; Smith, 2008). The implication behind studies focusing on such role holders is that those designated to lead are the only ones who count as leaders in universities.

Democratization of public discourse

Despite the focus of much of the literature on academic leadership in higher education, more generally there has been a reassessment and a democratization of opportunities for public discourse. A similar process is affecting modern day understandings of the intellectual. This is closely connected with changing social attitudes, the decline of deference toward professionals and the belief that everyone in society has an equal right to express an opinion. This means that it is not just those with a elevated position in the social hierarchy, such as academics, politicians, religious and business leaders, who are considered to have a legitimate voice on the basis of a superior education. Formerly, access to public communication channels was limited to the intellectual elite. If one wanted to be taken seriously and heard as an intellectual in a previous age it was essential to gain access to an audience through books, newspapers and radio and television stations. The educated members of the middle classes could write letters to newspapers or to their elected representatives. But the advent of the World Wide Web has opened up opportunities for anyone to communicate with large numbers of other people, bypassing elite communication channels. Personal websites, phone-in programmes on the radio, blogs, wikis and popular personal broadcast websites like YouTube mean that everyone can now compete for the attention of others on more equal terms (Cummings, 2005). While some intellectuals may bemoan the undermining of their authority in favour of the *vox populi*, others see this trend in more positive terms. Johnson (1988) argues that intellectuals have created climates of opinion and orthodoxies that have led to the justification of extremism. He contends that for intellectuals, concepts and ideas can matter more than people making them easily corrupted and happy to see lives sacrificed in pursuit of abstract philosophies. This makes them dangerous individuals who need to be kept away from influence in the corridors of power. Enabling the 'voice of the people' to be heard ensures that it is not just the views of a tiny elite that are aired.

Quite aside from the democratization of public discourse, there are several other reasons why the influence of the intellectual is said to have waned. Several books have appeared lamenting the decline of the intellectual in public life (e.g. Jacoby, 1987; Furedi, 2004). There are common elements to the narrative these and other books put forward. They include a belief that the professionalization of academia and the fragmentation of disciplines has led to fewer academics seeking to engage with wider audiences. Here, the 'temptation of the ivory tower' (Bourdieu, 1989, p. 660) and the division of knowledge into an increasing number of sub-disciplines means that academics stand accused of 'losing sight of anything outside one's immediate field' (Said, 1994, p. 57). University career and recognition systems tend to reward specialist research production rather than public engagement. There is also the perception that the modern role of the intellectual is as an interpreter or commentator on cultural trends rather than a more fundamental originator of new ideas (Bauman, 1987). Here, there has been a shift in power away from so-called mode 1 knowledge, created within academic disciplines, and toward mode 2 knowledge, more likely to be problem based and developed in the field of application (Gibbons *et al.*, 1994).

There has been a paradigmatic shift in the dominant way in which people think about the world. Sometimes this is referred to as postmodernism – the idea that all knowledge is socially constructed rather than universal in truth. The word constructivism is also invoked to mean much the same thing. Here it is argued that the world is just too complicated to know and that individuals without a specialist, or even real life, insight into particular cultures and environments are simply not qualified to comment. The truth depends on context; on language, nationality, religion and that all-encompassing word, culture. Universalism has been rejected in favour of relativism. The pursuit of universal laws of nature or sociological grand theories has become unfashionable. The only certainty in a postmodern analysis of the world is that what we know is individually and socially constructed and often based on the hegemony of Western cultural imperialism. The universal is no longer knowable. The American philosopher Richard Rorty has challenged the idea that philosophy can establish timeless truths, while Michel Foucault has similarly popularized cognitive relativism. As Furedi (2004) argues, 'today, the very possibility of knowing has been called into question' (p. 55). Those that try to be universalists, by asserting that there is a single standard or a principle that applies to all, go against the grain of postmodernism. Said (1994, p. 68) rails against the intolerance of relativism (or particularism) and the promotion of competing sets of values – Judeo-Christian, Afrocentric, Muslim, Eastern and Western truths – the result of which is 'an almost complete absence of universals' (p. 68). Hence, the shift to postmodernism undermines the conventional role of the intellectual in developing broad-based knowledge claims.

Illustrative of this cultural shift is the lionizing of so-called farmgate intellectuals (Boshier, 2002) who have significant achievements without the benefit of a formal or, perhaps, a higher education. University dropouts such as Richard Branson of Virgin, Steve Jobs of Apple or Bill Gates of Microsoft are held up as examples of individuals who have achieved great success in their fields of expertise without necessarily possessing the standard credentials of the intellectual. It is ironic that the 'university of life' is still so celebrated in a world that has seen a substantial increase in the provision of higher education. Clearly getting a university education is not a prerequisite for excelling in a variety of creative, artistic, commercial and intellectual pursuits. Most of the leading film-makers, theatrical performers and manufacturers from New Zealand, for example, have little or no formal higher education (Boshier, 2002). Clearly a shift has taken place towards a less elite model of public intellectualism. A degree of democratization has occurred as a result of the opportunities afforded by the World Wide Web and the emergence of intellectuals representative of a broader swathe of society and conventionally disenfranchised groups on the basis of race, gender and non-Western contexts.

Freedom and duty

So, the imagery might suggest that intellectual leadership is a phrase akin to 'resident alien' or 'genuine imitation'; essentially a contradiction in terms. But we need to get beyond the oxymoron if we are to progress in understanding what intellectual leadership means. My argument here, which will be developed further throughout the book, is that being an intellectual is essentially about *freedom*: in thinking and expression. In the university this is referred to as academic freedom. This involves being allowed the space to have ideas, experiment and take intellectual risks without interference. It is a licence to pursue lines of academic enquiry on the basis of personal dispositions and interests. This is granted because such freedom is thought to ultimately benefit society at large through the role of the university as its critical conscience and source of ideas.

The principle of academic freedom links closely with Wilhelm von Humboldt's argument that the state should leave the university alone as it is better served if allowed to fully develop its critical and research faculties. Hence, exercising academic freedom fully is one dimension of intellectual leadership in university life.

But academic freedom is not enough. Other qualities are needed to make an intellectual leader. Being a leader is also about taking on a *duty* to others. This involves selfless modes of behaviour; thinking about the needs of others, considering the effects of one's actions and giving up time one might prefer to spend on pursuing one's own intellectual interests. Within the academy, this is far less recognized but is just as important. When it is understood and valued it is referred to as service or academic duty (Kennedy, 1997; Macfarlane, 2007). Too often it is simplistically assigned the meaningless meta-label of 'administration' or 'management'. The distinction between academic freedom and academic duty is significant, since while each demands a different set of skills and attitudes they are essentially two sides of the same coin (Kennedy, 1997). You cannot have one without the other. To give a simple example, the freedom to pursue research depends, at least to some extent, on the duty to review articles for publication or evaluate grant proposals. If everyone asserted that their only role was to enjoy the freedom to research, who would manage the process of reviewing and editing the fruits of their labour? Hence, academic freedom and academic duty are mutually inter-dependent. This argument will be developed further later in the book (see Chapters 7 and 8) in linking certain characteristics or traits of intellectual leadership with the importance of balancing academic freedom and academic duty.

Being an intellectual leader in the context of university life requires an artful blend of the dispositions one might associate with academic freedom and academic duty. Enjoying the space to express a conceptual or theoretical view needs to be accompanied by actions that support others in their own endeavours, however modest. Of course, this does not necessarily imply that freedom and duty are unrelated. There are times when they are essentially one and the same, such as when persuading others on a course of action based on one's own thinking. Exercising the power of persuasion is about both freedom and duty; freedom of expression and the duty to lead through intellectual persuasion. Moreover, there is increasing understanding of the importance of this link beyond academia. Contemporary thinking about leadership is beginning to place more emphasis on the links between knowledge, wisdom and the act of leading (Rooney and McKenna, 2009). Wisdom is now recognized as critical to organizations obtaining a 'competitive advantage' from their own learning (Brown and Starkey, 2000). Leadership is about a lot more than 'managing' the day-to-day routine. It demands passion and commitment toward certain value-based goals such as environmental sustainability. The founder of the Body Shop, Anita Roddick, was someone who demonstrated that it was possible to combine business management with a commitment to social and moral causes including environmentalism.

Conclusion

The phrase 'intellectual leader' resonates but hides the tensions that lie in joining these words together. Cynics might contend the phrase is simply an oxymoron: that intellectuals do not make good leaders and that good leaders do not necessarily need to be intellectuals. Yet this cynicism is partly connected to a limited view of the nature of leadership. In practice, leadership can take many forms, and while intellectuals may be not be well equipped to undertake certain types of leadership role, they are better suited to others.

In an academic environment, intellectuals have many opportunities to lead as researchers, teachers and managers. Even here, however, the rise of managerialism has cast doubt on the role of academics as leaders. A professional model of university management has gathered pace, which has narrowed the intellectual basis upon which leadership is conceived. The role of those who might conventionally be considered to offer leadership by virtue of their intellectual credentials, notably full professors, has diminished. The chapter that follows will consider how the changing nature of the university has marginalized the role of professors as leaders.

Part 2

The entrepreneurial academy

Chapter 3

The retreat from engagement

Introduction

The modern university is a tough place. Despite popular imagery it is a long way from being an ivory tower detached from society. It is not a featherbed for unworldly individuals who cannot cope in the 'real' world. In reality, these kinds of metaphor are far from the truth. They are no longer true if, indeed, they ever were. Universities must compete for everything: students, especially those paying high fees from overseas; research funds; high calibre faculty members; political influence; business partners; gifts and donations; good publicity; and, above all, long-term survival. They are complex organizations with large budgets and valuable human and physical resources, constantly looking for ways to become more efficient. Moreover, this competitive environment is global, not just local or national. This belies the image of the monastic retreat.

Publicly funded universities, in all parts of the world, face increasing pressures to do more with less. They must try to offer mass, or perhaps universal, access to higher education with a lower unit cost. But at the same time they must respond to a broader social mission. Governments expect universities to meet the needs of multiple stakeholders: students, parents, professional bodies, taxpayers, business and industry and their own social and economic objectives. They must be all things to all people. The work of the university, its teaching and research, is scrutinized and audited. Judgements are made about its quality and conveyed via national quality audit regimes and international ranking tables. While offering crude, often narrowly construed and sometimes misleading snapshots of a more complex reality, these evaluations increasingly influence public perceptions, student decisions about where to study and government policy.

But here it is important to understand that these pressures are not unique to higher education. They represent an illustration of a broader theme affecting our society: the decline of trust in the public sector and in the professions. Doctors, social workers, the police and civil servants are similarly affected by overweening appraisal and performance systems reflected in endless league tables (Marquand, 2004). The loss of trust in the university can be seen both in terms of the changing nature of expectations directed at higher education and as part of a broader trend affecting the public sector. The modern university is expected both to encourage social justice and be globally competitive. This is a challenging dual social and economic expectation.

The growing divide

Part of the confusion that besets universities now is their own identity. There used to be a clear distinction between publicly and privately funded universities. Since the early twentieth century UK universities, for example, were largely supported by direct government grants. While the state has become a more 'hands-on' stakeholder since the latter part of the twentieth century, universities were still clear that they were benevolent institutions established for public benefit rather than private gain. However, the distinction between private and public universities has blurred. Governments, looking to extract better value for money, have started to make more public funding available to private higher educational providers. At the same time, publicly funded institutions have been encouraged to generate more of their income from private sources through entrepreneurial activity connected with research and teaching functions, including exploitation of intellectual property, recruiting more international students and establishing overseas campuses. Asking whether universities are public or private institutions might seem an odd question but the answer, that they are in fact both, is symbolic of the pressures they face to satisfy multiple stakeholders whilst maintaining traditions and practices associated with the history of the university.

In response to these pressures, universities have fundamentally changed the way in which they manage themselves. The collegial nature of decision making based on principles of consensus and academic rule have been replaced over the last 20 years by a managerial culture supported by a growing phalanx of professional support staff. Presidents (or vice chancellors) of these institutions define themselves as chief executives of large organizations rather than a first among equals or *primus inter pares*. They seek to maximize efficiencies, monitor and measure academic performance, and market the university's image. They are managers of large organizations. Yet most would still consider themselves principally as academics in identity and instinct. This is one of the tensions in the age of what has become known as 'new managerialism' (Deem and Brehony, 2005).

Part of this drive for efficiency has seen the slow pace of decision making in collegial systems of governance give way to an executive oligarchy based on managerial control. University senates have a reputation for being 'splendid at saying "no"' (Trow, 2010a, p. 446) and their declining influence is connected with the way that modern institutions recognize the importance of being more commercially nimble and market-responsive organizations. University management is now something that people *become* rather than *contribute to* whilst easily retaining a separate academic identity. Careers are no longer made in academia but in the sub-divided branches of teaching, research and management. This division of labour means that many of the functions that might formerly have been seen as part of the job of the all-round academic have been hived off (see Chapter 6). This trend has driven a wedge between those in academia who have continued to teach and research and those who have specialized in a career in academic management. University presidents, vice presidents, deans and heads of department are now more commonly permanent appointees rather than senior academics taking their rotational turn. It is hard for academic managers to return to the ranks due to the pace of change in academic disciplines. This is also connected to the way that management is now seen as a professional career choice rather than part of an older amateur tradition of reciprocal service.

In the UK, the publication of the *Jarratt Report* in 1985 (Committee of Vice Chancellors and Principals, 1985) marked a significant watershed in the shift of universities toward a more managerial ethos. The name of the committee that produced the report – the Standing Committee for Efficiency Studies in Universities – was an indicator of its intended effect. This was to increase the perceived efficiency and accountability of the sector. The report recommended that universities adopt a more managerial culture and shift power from departments to the corporate centre. The management function was seen by Jarratt as a 'self-justifying activity' (Becher and Kogan, 1992, p. 181) rather than something that was part of the historic dual role of academics.

The mid 1980s were a time when the philosophy of the free market had taken a strong hold in the political consensus in both the UK and the US, and when the perceived importance of reforming public services took root. In reality, governments of all political spectrums have continued to reform public services based on the same set of assumptions ever since. This is based on the idea that public services must strive for continuous efficiency gains and that the best way to achieve these is to replicate as far as possible the competitive conditions that apply to private sector organizations, including management techniques imported from this context. New managerialism has become the term associated with this set of assumptions. It is now widely accepted by politicians that public services must strive for continuous efficiency gains, and that the management practices of private industry offer the best means of achieving this goal. However, there are many in the academic profession who regard such new managerial practices in developing a highly competitive and performance-based environment as a threat to a cooperative ethic of academic identity (e.g. Waitere *et al.*, 2011).

Martin Trow (2010b) distinguished between two forms of managerialism in universities: 'soft' and 'hard'. He defined soft managerialism as an acceptance that managerial effectiveness is necessary for the proper functioning of universities, leading to a focus on the enhancement of efficiency. Here, a number of beliefs and aspirations come together, such as the desire to make universities less conservative and complacent, to forge stronger ties between academe and industry, and a desire to see higher education widen the basis of participation. Hard managerialism, by contrast, is based on the idea that academics cannot be trusted to govern their own affairs in a responsible manner and that, consequently, there is a need to apply business techniques to monitor and motivate their activities.

Trow recognized, at the time of writing in the early 1990s, that he was witnessing the triumph of hard managerialism. The assumptions underpinning hard managerialism are materially much the same as new managerialism characterized principally by the withdrawal of trust from the academic community (Trow, 2010b).

In universities the application of new managerialist philosophy has led to the increasing separation between management and academia. This is symbolized most clearly by the changing role of the professoriate within academic departments. In a UK context prior to the expansion of the system in the 1950s, the normal arrangement was for departments to be headed by a professor (Moodie, 1986). The comparatively small size of the university sector meant that departments tended to have just one professor who, as head of department, 'enjoyed absolute monarchy' (Becher, 1982, p. 73). Rotating the role of head of department only started when departments began, as a result of rising student numbers in the 1950s and 1960s, to contain more than one professor. Until the early 1960s, the role of professor and head of department was still virtually synonymous. In 1960–61, four-fifths of professors were heads of department (Halsey and Trow, 1971). Departments headed by someone other than a professor tended to be small or recently formed. Given the formerly influential role of professors as part of university senates a department without a professor as its head was at a serious disadvantage in terms of power and influence (Startup, 1976; Moodie, 1986).

Things started to change in the 1970s and 1980s, as first 'democratization' led to rotation of the role of the head among the whole department. Second, demands for universities to become more efficient and entrepreneurial in the 1980s meant that heads of department were faced with an even more demanding role. A role that had primarily been about leadership on the basis of being the pre-eminent scholar (Becher, 1982) had begun to develop into one that called upon a more complex set of managerial skills, such as recruitment of faculty, budgeting, marketing and strategic planning (Mathias, 1991).

This trend is widespread although it has taken longer to permeate university structures in some countries than others. The reform agenda in Germany has resulted in a more recent professionalization of university management, whereby self-governing academic decision making is being supplanted by more hierarchical and less participatory management structures (Vogel, 2009). The context is slightly different in Asia where governments, especially in countries such as China and Japan, have permitted more limited institutional autonomy, treating academics as civil servants rather than independent scholars. Hong Kong has long been seen as an exception to this norm and a comparative oasis of academic freedom (Currie *et al.*, 2006).

From scholar leader to manager

A career as a university leader or manager used to attract some of the most respected and distinguished scholars. University leadership, or 'administration' as it was more humbly termed, was seen as an important form of public service. A role as a university administrator was a key collegial duty and a respectable choice for a scholar often in the latter part of their academic career. An outstanding example of this tradition was Lord (Eric) Ashby. He enjoyed a successful career as a botanist, rising in the pre-war years through a series of academic positions at Imperial College, Bristol, and then the University of Sydney, where he became a professor at the tender age of 34. After the war he took another professorial position at the University of Manchester. In his mid-forties he became vice chancellor at Queen's University in Belfast, Northern Ireland spending nine years at the institution shaping its development at a critical time in its history. Ashby later became master of Clare College Cambridge and vice chancellor of the university toward the end of his career.

Ashby eschewed bureaucracy. Notably, as vice chancellor, his office had just one secretary. He focused instead on providing a strong academic infrastructure and good facilities in order to attract young, up-and-coming academics to Queen's. He was an accomplished and humorous writer and public speaker who insisted on handwriting his own reports, articles and speeches (Froggatt, 1992). Ashby was a vice chancellor though in an age when scholar leaders enjoyed a much greater degree of autonomy to shape their institutions in line with their own vision. While this term is frequently invoked in the management jargon of the modern age, it meant more in a time when reports and strategic statements were produced on rare occasions, at the initiative of the vice chancellor, rather than routinely required by state-funding bodies for higher education implementing increasingly interventionist policies. Not all university leaders of a past age were as engaging or charismatic as Ashby, but they had the space to make their own mark if they had the opportunity and ability.

But university leadership is a considerably less attractive career option for distinguished scholars in the contemporary age. A career in 'management' has become an earlier and more deliberate career choice, with many universities now encouraging premature specialization in teaching, research or management/ administration. There are now a new set of conventional expectations that university leaders will have risen through the ranks of managerial positions, from head of department, to dean, to vice president or pro vice chancellor, before necessarily being considered as a president or vice chancellor. An apprenticeship model has taken hold. This is hardly surprising given that institutions have become larger with more students, bigger budgets, heightened competition as the sector has expanded and internationalized, and more complex and demanding relationships with stakeholders. Leaders need business and commercial skills and these are beginning to displace the importance formerly attached to their personal scholarship (Burgan, 2006). Elite universities compete in a global market now. Management has become professionalized through training courses in leadership and masters' degrees in higher education management. This process of professionalization is perceived by academics as a necessary response to a rapidly changing, and more competitive, external environment for universities

(Locke, 2007). This does not mean, though, that academics seeking a scholarly career wish to engage with it. The all-consuming nature of university management and leadership means that there are fewer scholar leaders who are able to seriously maintain their research or teaching once appointed to a senior position. These expectations mean that academics have a more curtailed opportunity to forge a successful academic career and rise through the ranks before embarking on a managerial path.

Distinguished scholars are now less likely to be recruited to a senior leadership position directly from academe. The incentive for them participating, apart from monetary inducements, is also in decline for many of the reasons explained above – the lack of autonomy, the hugely demanding nature of the task, the professionalization of management and the expectation that other aspects of being an academic, notably being a researcher and a teacher, will need to be effectively abandoned. The global expansion of higher education and the corresponding market for intellectual talent worldwide also provides opportunities for distinguished faculty to continue their careers as visiting and honorary professors, consultants, advisors, writers and speakers well into official retirement. Despite efforts at national level to raise the status of teaching, the last 20 years has seen the interests of faculty shift steadily toward research and the more sharply individualized rewards it often brings in the way of prestige and career advancement. This is evidenced by an international survey of the changing nature of the academic profession, which reported that the proportion of academics primarily interested in teaching fell slightly (from 12 to 11 per cent) between 1992 and 2007, whereas over the same period those mainly motivated by research rose from 15 to 24 per cent (Universities UK, 2008).

The attractiveness of a leadership or management career is being further undermined by the growing lack of respect in which it is held. According to a different international survey, Australian academics are among the most dissatisfied with management (Coates *et al.*, 2010). This is ascribed by the authors to the ethos of new public management, otherwise known by the increasingly pejorative use of the terms management and managerialism. It is further the result of casualization of the academic profession that puts increasing pressure on faculty in continuing positions, and the huge growth in student numbers over the last two decades without a compensatory increase in staffing or other resources. Faculty members are also required to produce research that is fully funded, highly rated in terms of scholarship *and* has the potential to generate income. University management are associated with the embedding of this highly demanding set of performative expectations. The intensification of academic life is hence closely connected with the unpopularity of 'management' in an Australian context. Similar levels of discontent exist in a number of other national contexts, such as the UK.

Another important reason for the decline of respect and esteem for management is the sense that university leadership is now a pragmatic career choice rather than one prompted by a commitment to educational ideals. This does not mean to imply that contemporary managers and leaders do not have ideals and social commitments. What it does mean though is that becoming a manager used to involve sacrificing scholarly interests, for a period of time at least, in order to serve the wider academic community. It was about service rather than career. What we want from our leaders is the quality of selflessness. This is one of the seven principles of public life identified by the Nolan Committee on standards in public life (Nolan, 1997). Selflessness means that holders of public office should take decisions solely in terms of the public interest, and that they should not do so in order to gain financial or other material benefits for themselves, their family or their friends. Yet selflessness is about more than simply not being corrupt. It is about being dedicated to service rather than personal aggrandisement and personal gain. The focus on the pay of vice chancellors and other university leaders in recent times, demonstrating very often how their remuneration has risen faster in percentage terms than academics or other university employees, illustrates the declining sense of trust in the selflessness of university leaders.

A good example of a leader whose commitment to educational ideals was paramount was Patrick Nuttgens. After a successful academic career as an architect, Nuttgens became the founding director of Leeds Polytechnic in 1970. The founding principles of the polytechnics, as explained by Anthony Crosland, the British secretary of state for education in the mid 1960s, were to offer a distinctive form of higher education with strong community and industry links that promoted social mobility and provided greater access to part-time education (Whitburn *et al.*, 1976). The polytechnic ideal was one that greatly appealed to Nuttgens. He had previously moved from Edinburgh to York in the early 1960s to become one of York University's founding members. He also played a significant role in campaigning for the preservation of the city's architectural heritage. As a professor of architecture at Leeds University, and someone with a wide-ranging interests in the arts, Nuttgens could have chosen to have spent the best years of his career in a less challenging task. However, he was driven by a desire to connect the academic and the professional world more closely through his love of architecture and the practical arts, stemming partly from his background as the son of a stained glass artist. This made Nuttgens a great champion of the social and economic mission of the polytechnic, and he was keen to revive the ideal of the civic university by forging close industry links. This was a time in the UK when there was a stark, formal divide between the universities and the new polytechnics, and Nuttgens did much to break down the barriers between these alternate traditions despite the eventual conversion of the polytechnics into new universities in 1992.

Patrick Nuttgens was an outstanding polymath who opted for academic leadership as part of his commitment to trying to achieve his own educational ideals rather than as a pragmatic career choice. He was someone in the tradition of university leaders who continued to write and publish whilst acting in this role. There are other senior university managers who have maintained their academic profile despite the pressures of leadership. These include Derek Bok, who was president of Harvard for 20 years, David Watson, who was the vice chancellor of the University of Brighton for 15 years, and Peter Scott, the former vice chancellor of Kingston University. All these leaders continued to publish work during their time in office. Nowadays, though, the demands of university leadership mean that there are fewer role models who are able to combine their scholarship with managerial life. This has contributed to the growing sense of separation between academia and management. The examples of Ashby and Nuttgens also illustrate the way that what we mean by leadership in higher education has shifted away from the importance of symbolic and academic leadership (Trow, 2010a) and toward a more managerial form.

Pragmatic disengagement

The decline of the scholar leader at all levels of university management has contributed to the sense that academic identity is in crisis. A schism is said to exist between 'academic managers' and 'managed academics' (Winter, 2009). According to this thesis academic managers are those whose values are congruent with a managerial discourse about performance measurement, budgetary control and generating income. This is about a shift from a collegial to a corporate and entrepreneurial culture (Dopson and McNay, 1996). 'Managed academics' are forced to comply with this managerial discourse that they regard as an attack on the fundamental liberal values of the university including the pursuit of intellectual truth and knowledge as an end in itself.

While this argument contains an element of truth it would be too simplistic to suggest, as some have, that the university now contains 'academics' and 'managers' as two ideologically distinct and differently peopled groups locked in constant conflict. This is an exaggerated thesis. The reality, by contrast, is that academics and managers are more often than not one and the same and that 'academics continue to lead academics' (Smith, 2008, p. 349). The work of Smith (2008) reveals, for example, that over 80 per cent of those senior managers who occupy positions as pro-vice chancellors (the equivalent of vice presidents in the US) hold a professorial title. Moreover, this represents a continuous pattern of representation over 45 years. More members of the senior management teams of universities now possess a doctoral level qualification with around two-thirds holding a PhD or DPhil (Smith, 2008). The majority of heads of department in both 'old' and 'new' UK universities hold a doctorate (Sotirakou, 2004). These facts are not entirely consistent with the notion that academics have been excluded from the management of their own affairs. In fact, they point to their continuous and even more intimate involvement. While governance structures may now give a more powerful role to individuals external to the university, academics continue to largely control their own day-to-day affairs. The more complicated truth is that there are many academics in managerial positions who are uncomfortable with corporate rhetoric. At the same time the expansion of vocational subjects in universities means that an increasing number of academics are drawn from practice-based professions. These academics, who often continue to practice in heavily regulated professions, are more accustomed to the assumptions and expectations that underpin performance-based management.

The notion that academics have been replaced by an alternate cadre of professional managers is thus not entirely born out by the facts. The claims regarding the pernicious and coercive nature of managerialism are exaggerated (Klosaker, 2008). In many respects, academics have also contributed to the undermining of their own role and influence in the management of the university. As long ago as the early 1970s, professorial heads of department were themselves arguing that their managerial role should not necessarily be occupied by someone holding a professorial title (Startup, 1976). More recently, the false dichotomy between academics and management has sanctioned a further retreat from engagement among many academics. This is partly about an acceptance of some of the tenets of managerialism and the need for accountability. Indeed, it has been suggested that 'it may simply be that academics know no other way' (Kolsaker, 2008, p. 522). Academics have been pragmatic in 'reshaping' their professional identity in a way that often excludes responsibility for the management of their own affairs. This now means that 'academics are reasonably comfortable working with managerialist regimes and perceive little conflict between managerialism and academic professionalism' (Kolsaker, 2008, p. 519). This is underpinned by an instrumental attitude that managerialism, while distasteful, represents a necessary means to an end. It means that others are charged with administrative and managerial tasks many academics do not wish to undertake themselves. Instead, these pragmatic individuals focus on putting their energies into aspects of academic life that bring them more personal recognition and satisfaction, principally research and publication activity. Disengagement is about faculty members avoiding involvement in leadership and management of the institution and perceiving such activities as largely unappealing and unrewarding (Bolden *et al.*, 2009).

Global higher education institutions now keep an eager eye out for their latest world ranking according to either the QS World University Rankings or the Shanghai Jiao Tong. In a similar vein, academics working at such institutions have a tradeable value on the basis of intellectual metrics, which calculate their citation score and impact within their field of study. ISI web of science and Google scholar impact scores for publications are often quoted in contemporary academic CVs. Webometrics, as they are called, now rule. Academics have essentially complied with audit of research outputs in many national contexts by enthusiastically competing via such mechanisms and authenticating the results of such analysis through league tables and grade profiles. The process feeds personal egos and fits the often thinly disguised competitive nature of academic life. This is an example of what Nixon (2010a) terms a routine of complicity in higher education linked to an implicit acceptance of a market-based competitive framework, rather than one premised on the public good. This routine of complicity is an uncomfortable truth.

Hence, it is academics themselves who have, to some extent at least, chosen to disengage from the management of institutional life. The motivation for doing so cannot be entirely attributed to the increasing influence of a market-based philosophy in higher education. In part, it is about a diminishing ethic of service within a reshaped professional identity. Performative pressures linked to reward and recognition mechanisms have eroded the service ethic and produced a more self-centred culture focused on the pursuit of individual scholarly interests. This has been at the expense of taking an active role in the leadership of others, not just formally but informally, through activities associated with academic duty (see Chapter 8). It is also connected with the disaggregation of academic practice into separate component parts. Fewer and fewer academics teach, do research and provide service. Instead, they teach or research or provide service activities.

The management conundrum

My own research into the views of university professors indicates that they are divided about their role in university management (Macfarlane, 2011a). This involved the analysis of 233 responses to a questionnaire and 20 interviews about the role of a professor. Most responded that professors should lead and that this was part and parcel of their responsibility as professors. However, quite a large minority stated that professors do not necessarily make good academic managers and that the roles of professor and manager should be separated. Some argued that the two roles demand different skill sets, whilst others regarded managerial responsibilities as an unhelpful distraction for professors who should focus their energies on research and intellectual leadership:

> It always puzzled me that skills at getting grants and publishing papers should be interpreted as 'this person would be good at running a department', which is quite a different job. It is a mistake lots of universities make.
>
> (professor of engineering)

> I don't think professors should run the department, because then they will never do the things they are supposed to do which is research and intellectual leadership.
>
> (professor of philosophy)

One of the problems though of dividing these roles is credibility. According to a meta-analysis of the literature on academic leadership, credibility is key (Bryman, 2007). Possessing a credible scholarly profile gives someone face validity to manage academics. Therefore, appointing managers or leaders without a professorial title was seen as problematic, particularly when these people would be expected to manage senior academics:

> Professors at my institution are primarily leaders and role models, and are not necessarily 'management'.
>
> (professor of oncology)

A professor should be an intellectual leader and his/her authority stems entirely from this.

(professor of economics)

Possessing an established academic reputation as a researcher was seen by those professors that I interviewed as a big advantage in this context. As one professor of English told me 'you don't get taken seriously [as a head of department] if you are not a professor'.

Those appointed as a professor mainly on the basis of service to the institution through carrying out managerial responsibilities were not generally regarded as 'legitimate' professors:

... there are some people who have been given professorships ... who should never have them, because they are for absurd things, such as being head of department for years ... or for having sat on an unconscionable number of committees. That's also a very bad reason.

(professor of English)

The importance of leaders being professors in universities has led some institutions to conflate the professorial title with senior managerial roles. One interviewee argued that UK universities created in 1992 as a result of the conversion of the polytechnics had tended to 'abuse' the professorial title by conferring it on 'anybody in any position of hierarchical seniority', such as deans or pro-vice chancellors. This, it was argued, was a symptom of a lack of confidence among such institutions and unhelpfully conflated two distinct roles. Another interviewee argued that in the post-1992 university in which he worked there was a legacy of having made too many internal appointments to professorial chairs:

I suspect that because this is a new university and it has changed its status that some of the initial appointments [i.e. as professors] were not very good appointments and they may have been internal appointments because they had to have professors ... just appointing someone internally because they are a good chap and they have been in the set up for a number of years is wrong.

(professor of law)

Several professors I spoke with also referred to tensions that can exist when they are managed by a head of department or dean who does not hold a professorial title or possess a substantial research profile:

... if you are being managed by staff who are junior to you by virtue of their curriculum vitae etc., it puts both individuals I think in a very difficult position, a very embarrassing position.

(professor of history)

Where a head of department or dean is not a professor it can create practical problems in managing professorial faculty. An obvious example is performance-based review or evaluation. In this situation the head of department may not be seen as a legitimate judge, resulting, in some institutions, in the responsibility being handed to a different senior manager, sometimes the vice chancellor, who is a professor. Hence, while it might seem sensible to argue that managerial and professorial roles are in some ways distinctive and to therefore disassociate them from each other, the reality is complex. The importance of credibility means that it is better if those occupying senior managerial positions in universities are also professors in their own right. This gives them a face validity to lead and manage. It does not make them necessarily good leaders but it provides them with a much-needed point of first identity.

Conclusion

Despite the march of a market-based philosophy, the leadership of the academy is still largely in its own hands. In other words, we have no one to blame but our-selves if we do not like how we are being led and by what set of values and objectives. There still exists the opportunity to develop a new form of intellectual leadership that offers an alternate vision to the divisive dichotomy between aca-demic managers and managed academics. As part of my contribution to this alternative vision I will outline the qualities of intellectual leadership in the chapters that follow in Part 3 of the book. There still remains though the ques-tion as to how to reestablish the role of the professoriate in the leadership of the university. While this has not yet been lost there is a risk that the retreat from engagement will continue. This needs to change if the professoriate is to meet the challenge of managerialism.

Chapter 4

The corporatization of the research agenda

Introduction

This book is mainly concerned with the characteristics that make intellectual leaders. The focus, in other words, is on individuals. However, one might also legitimately assert that universities, as organizational entities, have a role to play in offering intellectual leadership. The way that they choose to present themselves in this respect has been reinvented under the umbrella of 'knowledge transfer' or 'knowledge exchange'. This is sometimes spoken of as the new third 'leg' of the university mission. While teaching, research and service have long been acknowledged as the mainstream purposes of the university (Cummings, 1998), in recent years service as an essentially benign, *pro bono* activity has evolved into something more closely related to meeting the economic needs of wider society.

The terms principally associated with this shift toward a more 'entrepreneurial university' (Barnett, 2003) are knowledge transfer and knowledge exchange. Knowledge transfer suggests that universities have intellectual assets that they can share with society resulting in a range of applications for social and economic betterment. Knowledge exchange is perhaps a more enlightened phrase, since it implies that this process is not simply one way and that universities can also learn from knowledge generated in the context of application. Yet both phrases symbolize the way in which the university's activities can contribute to the development of knowledge in wider society and are linked to the commercialization and corporatization of academic labour.

Unfortunately these attempts to redefine, or perhaps reassert, the mission of the university have adverse consequences for intellectual freedom at the individual level. Here, personal scholarly agendas have given way to corporate alignment and the corralling of academics into research 'strands', 'clusters' and other groupings. These are intended to represent directions perceived as beneficial for the wider organizational mission and commercial interests. In this chapter I will argue that the redirecting of research and scholarly interests in this manner is resulting in a corporatization of intellectual leadership, which is counter-productive to originality and creativity in academic life.

University research themes

Nearly all major universities now have institutional-wide research themes with a sub-structure of faculty- and departmental-based themes underpinning these objectives. A good example of the corporatization of intellectual leadership is provided by University College London, one of the world's foremost research universities. It has identified what it terms as four 'grand challenges' that all its research and scholarly efforts are directed at meeting: global health, sustainable cities, intercultural interaction and human wellbeing (University College London, 2011). Other universities around the globe have their own sets of themes or challenges. The University of Hong Kong (2011), for example, has five research areas and 19 strategic research themes. These include cancer, healthy ageing, sustainable environment and China–West studies. The last of these themes is indicative of the way that institutions seek to reflect regional and localized concerns within their selection of themes. The University of Auckland (2011) in New Zealand includes 'Indigenous "Knowledges", Peoples and Identities' as one of its three strategic research initiatives, reflecting the local cultural context and in some ways seeking to redress historically endemic discriminatory practices. Similarly, in Canada concerns about the treatment of, and respect for, the cultures of Aboriginal peoples means that a leading research university such as Simon Fraser includes 'Origins' among a list of six research themes (Simon Fraser University, 2010). The university's other themes also have a strong emphasis on culture, the environment and human health. The move to majority rule in South Africa following the post-apartheid era means that issues such as democracy and human rights are prominent issues in this context. Hence, it is not surprising to see this concern together with others related to African society in the five research themes identified by the University of Stellenbosch (2011): eradicating poverty and related conditions; promoting human dignity and health; promoting democracy and human rights; promoting peace and security; and promoting a sustainable environment and a competitive industry.

Whilst university themes often reflect national and local concerns, they tend to cluster around the big global issues of today such as environment and technology, health and disease, conflict and insecurity, poverty and development, and developing a better understanding of culture and cultural difference. University research themes are presented as part of a university's commitment to the betterment of society. They are an integral means by which universities seek to market and differentiate themselves in an increasingly crowded market. It is also important to realize, however, that university research themes tend to have a bias toward science and technology partly as these areas of research are likely to generate more income for the institution through grants from governments, research councils and charitable and private organizations, including pharmaceutical companies. This is perhaps illustrative of the way that money has come to replace knowledge as the key driver of universities (Brennan, 2011). It is also representative of the triple helix whereby research is now seen as about the interconnection of the interests of universities, industry and government (Etzkowitz and Leydesdorff, 2000). Research themes associated with disciplines that are less likely to generate large-scale funding, mainly in the arts, humanities and social sciences, tend to be fewer by comparison. Hence, university research themes tend to have a science and technology bias despite their apparently interdisciplinary nature. They are also invariably agreed upon at a senior level or by a research committee as part of a strategic approach to university research.

Part of the idea of having research themes is to cluster together researchers in groups that might have more critical mass and subsequent impact on theory and practice as a result. Many middle ranking universities cannot afford to invest in and support research activities across the full spectrum of disciplines. Research themes are a way for institutions to market themselves to the wider world and assert their role in society for public benefit. Additional support is often available for academics doing research that directly feeds into a theme. Internal research support may indeed depend on any project being explicitly linked to a research theme. Hence, themes often look to address contemporary issues facing society, such as those identified by the University of Hong Kong. Few would argue with the need for promoting greater understanding across cultures in a globalized world, improving public health care and finding treatments for cancer and Alzheimer's disease, or looking for ways to tackle environmental degradation and using up less of the earth's remaining natural resources.

Ostensibly then the identification of research themes is a good thing since they provide a clear sense of organizational direction or mission and demonstrate how universities add value to society. In part they are prompted by pressures on modern institutions to justify their public funding and establish a clear sense of their role in contemporary society. They are focused on research areas that reflect current trends and concerns rather than less fashionable topics with more limited capacity to generate funding or institutional recognition. Furthermore, as I argued in Chapter 1, universities are no longer unchallenged as knowledge producers and must compete for attention in a more democratic and open network of communications where information is freely available over the internet. They have a 'diminishing monopoly of expertise' (Arnoldi, 2007, p. 49). This is why universities now have communications officers and knowledge transfer offices as they vie with an array of other knowledge-producing and opinion-setting organizations and individuals.

Political correctness

However, university research themes contain a strong element of political correctness. This is closely connected with the scripted communication designed to imply commitment to a set of sacred principles, whether one believes in them or not (Lea, 2009). The University of Hong Kong has China–West Studies as one of its strategic research themes. This is reflective of a number of other universities in the UK, Canada, the US, Australia and elsewhere who choose to focus on an exploration of cultural difference. Arguably, this promotes the notion of East and West as a dualism and results in the 'othering' of the East and West as if this were the only explanatory framework for global divisions (Cousin, 2011). This dualism has become a form of political correctness since to dispute its validity is seen as disrespectful of cultural differences. Interest in exploring this divide stems, to some extent, from Edward Said's work and notably his 1985 book *Orientalism* (Said, 1985). This provoked a worldwide debate about representations of West and East. Like other strategic research themes identified by universities and research councils though, it is based on what is already (thought to be) known and important, or what is essentially part of the conventional discourse of academic life, rather than encouraging new boundaries to be transgressed or contrary ideas to emerge. Researchers in these thematic areas are essentially seen as serving or contributing to the theme rather than challenging the legitimacy of the prescribed research agenda.

Hence, research themes focus on issues that are perceived to be of contemporary relevance to society. This focus contrasts with research that is curiosity based and often theoretically driven, and which does not have any immediate, obvious application. Such work is sometimes referred to as blue skies research. Arguably, though, blue skies research can produce benefits to society on the basis of needs it currently cannot identify or anticipate. However, despite the historic role of more curiosity-driven scholarship in academic life, the economic 'impact' of research is something that academics are now routinely asked to identify by research councils and other grant-making bodies. It means that academics are rewarded for research activities that are perceived to be adding to our stock of knowledge or insight connected with a preexisting theme, rather than being encouraged to take an intellectual lead themselves. Moreover, themes do not encourage disputation as they take as a given the correctness of certain beliefs and paradigms, such as environmental protection or understanding cultural differences.

An even more worrying practice is connected with the role of governments in setting research themes on the basis of party political agendas. In the UK, the minister for universities and science has stated that it is appropriate for ministers to ask research councils how they can contribute to the government's national priorities (Jump, 2011). This expectation has allegedly led to the inclusion of the government's stated desire for a so-called 'Big Society' being included as one of the Arts and Humanities Research Council's strategic priorities (Jump, 2011). This kind of direct or indirect political interference in the setting of research priorities is in marked contrast to the Haldane principle. This refers to the idea that research councils should be autonomous and free from government direction in how to spend research funds. This principle has helped to ensure that academic researchers, rather than politicians, should determine how to best spend research funds, and was established as a result of a report produced by Richard Haldane published in 1918 (Haldane Report, 1918). While some contend that the Haldane principle is a myth (Edgerton, 2009), the concept of freedom of research that is free from government direction has a strong tradition, regardless of the extent to which the principle is a myth or a reality.

A very different philosophy is represented in Germany, where research institutes exist outside the university system. Here, the Max Planck institutes have been long established as non-governmental and non-profit making centres for research excellence. They are focused on basic research in the natural sciences, life sciences, social sciences and the humanities. Individual academics in these research institutes define their own agenda for academic enquiry rather than being directed by corporatized research themes. They focus on research fields that are particularly innovative, or that are especially demanding in terms of funding or time requirements and have helped to generate 32 Nobel Prizes. However, it needs to be acknowledged that considerable power in such institutes tends to rest with the vision of directors of research areas rather than necessarily with individual researchers.

Exploiting intellectual property

While universities need to engage with society and demonstrate social as well as economic value, there are further, negative consequences to the corporatization of intellectual leadership. One of these is the way that universities are keen to protect, and exploit for commercial gain, the intellectual property rights of work carried out by academics in the course of their employment. The focus on commercialization means that institutions are now increasingly evaluating academic research for its applied potential rather than theoretical or conceptual value. Academic research comes in many different forms and disciplinary entities, not all of which have a commercial application. The work of scholars in the arts, humanities and some of the social sciences is therefore, in particular, under pressure to justify research in terms of its commercial value and impact. Here, there is potentially dissonance between the norms of a discipline, particularly where this is not focused strongly on applied settings, and the research agenda that academics are expected to follow. Academic enquiry is no longer disinterested. It needs to demonstrate a clear line of eventual relevance to societal needs or it runs the risk of being labelled as self-indulgent and irrelevant. Those academics able to fit their research around the current research themes are likely to receive more institutional support and attention. Those who do not meet this expectation may be ignored, marginalized or even fired. This promotes conformity rather than individuality as the quality that is appreciated and rewarded in the modern university.

Other distortions to intellectual endeavours result from corporatization. One of the most worrying is the way that it has transformed the role of the academic. Personal scholarly interests now take second place to pursuing research funding opportunities and a focus on research topics that are topical and perceived as relevant to contemporary concerns, however fleeting and inconsequential. While the value and quality of research and scholarly efforts has conventionally been judged solely by reference to the discipline, it is now audited by universities and governments in terms of its ability to generate revenue for the university, citations from other academics and a measurable, immediate impact on wider society. The problem of corporatization of the research agenda for the individual academic is neatly summarized by Thorens (2006, p. 100):

> The researcher who wishes to pursue or undertake research in an unfashionable field, one totally new or of no economic interest can thus sometimes be penalized and may even abandon his project to undertake 'recognized' research, which will help his career and advance his being 'recognized'.

Hence, the academic is an increasingly market-driven actor (Gordon, 2010) who must compete for funding and justify her or his intellectual activities while disseminating their 'message' in the crowded world of the multi-media. There is stronger international competition for leading research academics amongst the emerging elite of global universities and an active transfer market (Wildavsky, 2010). The risk here is that unfashionable research that fails to fit the populist or corporate agenda, but may pay future dividends in an unpredictable world, may be lost to society.

This environment is breeding a short-termism in intellectual thought and activities bolstered by an increasingly global academic labour market, which judges the quality of intellectual achievement by the yard. Measurement takes the form of the monetary value of research awards, the numbers of publications and, critically, citation counts. The emphasis on citation counts as a supposedly objective measure of academic achievement and impact overlooks the distortions such a system creates. Aside from the risk of unscrupulous or simply calculative individuals establishing cliquish citation rings, where common agreement is reached between several close academic colleagues to cite each other, citation counts encourage academics to research and publish in already established or popular fields. This means that an average scholar writing in a popular field has an in-built advantage over the more talented, and perhaps unconventional, scholar writing in a less popular field, since the former is more likely to be subsequently cited by their more numerous peers. Citation analysis is a disincentive to be different and to try to forge new intellectual directions. It is an incentive to toe the line, to fit in with existing strands of thought and analysis, and contribute to fields where there is already burgeoning activity.

These developments represent an erosion of what is sometimes referred to as disinterested research: that which is not prompted by responding to the agendas as set by others such as research funding bodies, charities, corporations, governments or universities themselves. Disinterested research is not just about scholarly self-direction. It is further related to academics having no vested interest in the outcome of research in the sense that it corresponds with particular predispositions or biases. This is important to protect as where funded research is undertaken, academics are often keenly aware of the political, social and economic expectations of those that have commissioned the work. Researchers who concluded that passive smoking was not a serious health risk were much more likely to have received funding from tobacco companies for their work (Barnes and Bero, 1998). Moreover, unethical behaviour to please the sponsoring organization is not such a rare or isolated problem as is sometimes assumed. In a survey of academics who had received funding for research from a funding body, 15 per cent admitted that they had altered some aspect of the research, including the findings (Martinson *et al.*, 2005).

Disinterestedness is one of the four key values of academic life originally identified by Robert Merton (1942). Unfortunately, disinterestedness is a luxury the modern academic cannot afford, since they need to have a constant and vigilant eye to the outcome and impact of scholarly endeavour. One of the other values identified by Merton was communism, a word that carries an emotive and sometimes pejorative meaning in a political context. However, in an academic arena Merton used the term to refer to the disposition among academics to freely share intellectual ideas and discoveries, a process sometimes also labelled as the intellectual commons (Halsey and Trow, 1971). This process is not just about good manners or a generosity of spirit. It is about a common commitment to a process of intellectual advancement, a sharing of ideas for an end that benefits everyone: human progress. This is more important than bolstering the ego of the individual scholar by that person being able to claim that he or she is the first to make a breakthrough or discovery. It is also, or should be, more important than material gain or commercial benefits. However, universities routinely agree to restrictions being placed on the disclosure of scientific advances by commercial sponsors, notably pharmaceutical companies. Rather than disseminate results they are kept hidden to ensure that no one else may steal a march on potential profits to be gained from a new drug.

Training for corporate ends

The development of researchers (or 'researcher development') is an increasing area of university activity coming in the wake of efforts to improve the quality of teaching via faculty or educational development over the last 20 years. The research councils have been influential in encouraging this work, resulting in a growth of formal training programmes (Gordon, 2005). Doctoral students, and academic faculty without strong or productive scholarly records, are the principal targets of research development. In the UK, Vitae, an arm of the Careers and Advisory Research Centre (CRAC) supported by the research councils, works to embed professional and career development for researchers. A new researcher development statement was published by Vitae in 2010, as agreed by the various research councils replacing the Joint Skills Statement as the main point of reference for university training of researchers (CRAC, 2011).

One of the more troublesome aspects of the researcher development statement is its conflation of generic aspects of training (such as research methods) with attitudinal expectations designed to reinforce corporate purposes. These include 'global citizenship', 'society and culture' and 'enterprise'. While these dispositions are presented as 'knowledge and skills' they are, in reality, corporate mantras, attitudes and values that are closely connected with the marketing of higher education institutions. They further connect with university research themes that, as shown earlier in this chapter, champion a range of politically correct public policy priorities.

The legitimation of corporate purposes by the researcher development statement is part of a broader process of training to meet institutional needs rather than encourage intellectually autonomous academic practitioners. In some respects it mirrors the way in which postgraduate certificates in learning and teaching for academic faculty seek to combine generic theory associated with student learning with the inculcation of institutional policy (Macfarlane, 2011b).

Conclusion

The corporatization of the research agenda is adversely affecting the quality of academic life and the extent to which academics are free to define and pursue their own research and scholarly agenda. While they may not be directly prevented from exercising this privilege, contemporary rewards and incentives encourage conformance with the research agenda of universities, research councils, business organizations, charities and governments. Academics place a particular value on autonomy or independence to establish and pursue their own scholarly direction. This is critical to why many choose to pursue an academic career in the first place, sometimes forgoing more lucrative career opportunities to apply their expertise in the commercial sector. Those that research and write about what motivates academics frequently refer to the centrality of autonomy (Feldman and Paulsen, 1999).

Moreover, the privilege associated with the freedom of enquiry on the basis of personal scholarly interests may appear arcane and essentially selfish, but indirectly supports research that is based on principles that benefit society the most. These are that it is conducted in a disinterested manner and the results are freely shared for the benefit of further advancement. Intellectual advancement demands a commitment to these values, which the mission of the entrepreneurial university undermines. Here there is a need for universities to reassert their role as intellectual leaders and create the right environment for individuals with creativity and curiosity to prosper. Being clear what a university stands for is the starting point in offering intellectual leadership. This is a theme I will seek to address later in the book by reference, in part, to the way that many universities are now seeking to exploit the financial rewards of an expanding global higher education system (see Chapter 10).

Freedom and duty

Part 3

Freedom and duty

Chapter 5

Becoming a professor

Introduction

Who is a professor and how does someone become one? This chapter will focus on answering this question. In doing so, I will begin to draw more on my research into how professors see their role in universities today, including their experience of the appointment process. While most universities have relatively similar formal standards connected with becoming a professor, it is important to understand that there is also considerable tacit organizational knowledge related to this process. In other words, what is written down needs to be supplemented with an understanding of the practice, as well as the theory. Criteria are often framed in quite a generalized way, referring to 'scholars of international standing' or those possessing a 'significant impact' or 'reputation' in an academic field. Such phraseology is common but requires interpretation. This means that the appointment process is still shrouded, to some extent, in rumour and legend, requiring tacit professional knowledge in order to decipher it.

The chapter will further consider the way in which the appointment standards appear to be shifting in response to the changing nature of the university and the way its function is altering. Here, there is now a stronger emphasis on achievements in research as opposed to excellence in other elements of the academic role, such as teaching and service contributions. Furthermore, one notable feature of this change is a perception among professors that, regardless of discipline, income generation, in addition to publication, is now of heightened significance in meeting institutional expectations.

Who is a professor?

One would have thought it should be relatively easy to establish who a professor is but in fact it is remarkably difficult to give a simple answer to this apparently simple question. This is because the use of the term 'professor' varies considerably across national contexts and there are different traditions that determine who can call themselves one. It is a slippery term.

In some contexts, such as Latin America, it is commonplace to refer to teachers at all educational levels as a 'professor'. A professor in Spanish can also mean a secondary school teacher. The use of the term is liberally applied in the United States and Canada to both teachers and academics working in post-secondary education. Yet most North American professors are really employed as instructors, lecturers or teaching assistants. Here, a real professor is generally recognized as someone who has risen in academic rank in a university to the position of 'full' professor, as distinct from the more junior positions of assistant and associate professor.

In the UK and mainland Europe, a more restrictive and legally defined use of the term 'professor' applies. In Germany, forging an academic career and eventually becoming a professor is a lengthy and arduous process. After completing a doctorate, a budding academic must work toward something called 'habilitation' by writing a second thesis, normally whilst employed in a junior university position. Once someone has passed their habilitation they are called a Privatdozent, known as a docent or dosent in several other countries. Only after this position is reached would someone be eligible for a chair (i.e. a professorial position), although in some German states a minimum five-year qualification period as a Privatdozent is required. With some differences, a relatively similar situation applies in France and Scandanavian countries, like Finland. In the UK, there is no absolute requirement that a professor must possess a doctorate, and it is common in some applied and professional disciplines for professors not to have one. The nomenclature also differs and ranks below that of (full or chair) professor are normally referred to as lecturer, senior lecturer or principal lecturer in post-1992 universities.

Globalization is having many effects on society, and this includes the spread of the American model of the university. In recent years, some UK universities, such as Warwick, have begun to adopt North American nomenclature referring to academic ranks as assistant, associate and then full professor. This is also common parlance in Asia, where British influence in former colonial contexts, like Hong Kong, has waned and the North American terminology is now applied. Normally professors at all levels – assistant, associate and full – are professionally autonomous, although in Japan, up until a new law was passed in 2007, assistant and associate professors were primarily required to support the work of full professors. The change in the law, however, does not automatically mean that the established behaviour patterns of assistant and associate professors in Japan will alter. It may take several generations before the cultural practice aligns with the new legal position.

There is also the question of tenure. This means that a professor, or indeed an academic of a lower rank, may hold her or his position as a lifetime privilege until retirement. This is a major area of interest and concern in academic life that affects career patterns, mobility and job security. Notably, tenured positions are on the decline in the United States and several other national contexts, influenced by the perceived need among senior management and governments for a more flexible and responsive higher education system. Despite popular imagery, being an academic is one of the more insecure occupations of modern times. For example, there are large numbers of so-called adjunct professors in the US, referring to academic appointees without a permanent university position. However, while a tenure system applies in some countries, notably the US, it is far from universal and does not apply in the UK and Australia, for example.

A distinction is often drawn between professors who hold personal chairs and those with established (or endowed) chairs. Personal chairs are awarded to an academic who has achieved scholarly distinction in any field, and are generally the most common way that someone might become a professor. Once the individual leaves the university, for whatever reason, the professorial position or chair that they have occupied does not continue to exist. An established chair, by contrast, is one endowed by a sponsor for an indefinite period and would be expected to offer leadership in their subject. Such positions would normally carry more prestige than personal chairs and possibly a higher salary as a result of being established through a legacy or some form of corporate or charitable sponsorship.

Levels of remuneration for professors can vary considerably between types of institution, and are also dependent on the scarcity of or demand for professors in particular disciplines. Where professors are capable of generating considerable revenues or there is competition for their services from the private sector, in cutting edge pharmaceutical research or in some business specialisms, a market premium tends to apply. Figures from the American Association of University Professors shows that, at the most extreme, the average salary of a full professor in the business, administration and management field is 58 per cent higher than for an equivalent colleague in the fine arts (AAUP, 2011a).

Clearly not all professors enjoy equal status, by reference to both income and prestige, within as well as across higher education systems or individual universities. Status further relates to the types of roles that are undertaken by professors. In China, for example, only more experienced professors are permitted to become PhD supervisors, a restriction that is not commonly found in other contexts. Someone seeking to become a *bodao* (i.e. one permitted to supervise PhD candidates) must be approved by a university committee charged with assessing their academic credentials (Yuchen, 2007).

A great deal of prestige is attached to the title of regius professor, available in a small number of ancient universities in the UK and Ireland. These are appointments originally created by a monarch and may be found at a number of ancient institutions, including the universities of Oxford, Cambridge, Dublin, Glasgow, St Andrews, Aberdeen and Edinburgh (Hogg, 2007). The crown still needs to approve new appointments, with the exception of Dublin since Irish independence. Mostly regius professorships are in 'traditional' university subjects such as anatomy, divinity, Greek, medicine and modern history.

There are also honorary professors, a title bestowed on a variety of public figures from the world of academe, politics, sport and entertainment. However, these individuals are not in any real sense a professor, as they do not carry out academic work associated with the title, at least not normally at the awarding university. Appointing an honorary professor is seen as an important element of the marketing and promotion of modern universities. Occasionally, an honorary professor might give a guest lecture but, essentially, this is a purely honorific title without carrying teaching or research responsibilities.

The term emeritus professor is reserved for retired professors who are still active in their scholarly field, and is normally granted by an institution to former employees who have reached the rank of full professor during their term of employment. Emeritus professors often continue to fulfil roles as university teachers, researchers and supervisors on a part-time basis. The status and role of emeritus professors though is poorly articulated (Thody, 2011). I will argue later in the book that institutions need to revisit how they utilize the skills and expertise of these 'retired' scholars (see Chapter 11).

Hence, there is a very wide range of traditions associated with the term professor. Linguistically, the word professor often translates as teacher. In Chinese, a university professor is called a *Dàxué jiaoshou*. In practice, a professor is often addressed as *jiaoshou*. The characters for *jiao* and *shou* both have meanings connected with teaching. This observation is not without significance, since it denotes the principal historic role of university professors (and other ranks) as teachers rather than researchers. Halsey and Trow's study of British academics during the 1960s found that only 10 per cent were interested in research, and a mere 4 per cent regarded research as their first duty (Halsey and Trow, 1971). Writing in the late 1970s, Wilson (1979) asserts that the majority of American academics considered 'teaching to be more important than research' (p. 234). While we might now assume that the professorial title is most closely associated with research and scholarship, it was not always so. Like so many other traditions, what it means to be a professor has been reinvented. Hence, the contemporary dominance of the research role is relatively recent.

The trend toward a stronger focus on empirical research, in particular, is a function of a number of factors, including the expansion of the higher education system. This has led elite institutions to look to new ways to differentiate themselves from access-based providers who are focused more strongly on widening participation and concentrate on teaching rather than research. Over the last 20 years there has been an exponential growth in professional development for academic faculty, in response to the massification of higher education and increasing competition between institutions for students, both nationally and internationally. A wide range of reward and recognition schemes to promote interest in, and respect for, the teaching role have been introduced such as institutional and nationally based prizes for teaching excellence in countries such as the US, Canada, Australia and the UK. Considerable efforts have been made to promote the scholarship of teaching and learning in the wake of Boyer's influential work (Boyer, 1990). However, despite all these initiatives to raise the status of teaching, international survey data indicates that the professional priorities of the academic profession have shifted in the *opposite* direction, towards research rather than teaching (Universities UK, 2008).

Mass higher education has brought increasing stratification between institutions as well as between individual academics within them. Formally many university systems, such as those in Australia and the UK, are unitary rather than binary, inasmuch as there is no legal or technical distinction between different types of university or higher education provider. However, in practice universities compete in different markets, for different types of students and for different sorts of resources supporting teaching and research. The research elite universities have more diversified income streams and often enjoy support from wealthy sponsors. Access-based institutions must rely heavily on income from government, and to some extent tuition fees, on the basis of their teaching activities.

At the individual level, this differentiation is reflected by the way that the academic role is splintering into specialist pathways. Academic faculty can now be placed on three or more career tracks such as teaching only, research and teaching, or management. Even where this does not occur formally, it can occur informally as academics choose the direction of their career. In a highly differentiated and performative environment, being able to do it all as an academic all-rounder is clearly more challenging. The proportion of faculty employed in teaching-only positions has increased, and the disaggregation of the role into teaching, research and management career tracks means that academic life is now more differentiated into the haves and have-nots. Crudely, the haves mainly work in elite institutions, do research and spend comparatively little time teaching. The have-nots mainly work in access-based institutions, do little or no research, and spend most of their time teaching and assessing students (Sikes, 2006). In practice the situation of academics is more nuanced than this, inasmuch as there are research-tracked faculty members in access-based institutions, and teaching or management-focused ones in research-based universities. Hence, the relative status of the institution is only an indicator, albeit a strong one, of relative opportunities.

The fragmentation of academic work means that professors are not necessarily all-rounders anymore, expected to teach, research *and* perform leadership or management roles. In other words, like other faculty, they might specialize in just one element of academic practice such as teaching, research or management. This is a process sometimes labelled unbundling, and has resulted in an increasing use of adjectives like 'research professor' and, occasionally, 'teaching professor' to denote someone's principal role. The unbundling of academic roles is changing what it means to be a professor or indeed an academic more generally (see later in this chapter).

Getting appointed

The shifting nature of professional priorities is reflected in the standards that are applied in appointing someone to a chair or full professorship. Despite institutional rhetoric claiming an equal valuing of teaching, service or knowledge transfer activities, in practice the research profile of the individual is the dominant criterion rather than other aspects of their work.

The formal criteria for becoming a professor may be found in the appointment and promotions information issued by most university human resources departments.

This normally centres on an individual demonstrating that they have acquired a national and/or, more usually, international reputation for the quality of their research and scholarship. This is often expected to be evidenced by peer-reviewed publications, the acquisition of research grants, contributions to academic and professional bodies and other impact measures in shaping the conceptual or applied thinking or practice of others. Impact measures might include things like citation rates or honours associated with intellectual recognition, such as serving on national committees, advising government ministers or heading prestigious scholarly societies. The following statement from the UK's University of Sussex (2008) is not untypical in reflecting this multiple set of expectations:

> Candidates for promotion to a Professorship will be expected to have made a broad, sustained contribution to their field and discipline nationally and internationally, and normally to have achieved exceptional performance in research. Demonstrated leadership in the development of teaching in their subject and field may play a dominant part in a case. Service to their subject, to the University and to higher education in administrative or research capacities may contribute to the case.

Others have sought to summarize the essential qualities needed to become a professor. In a 1991 document the UK-based National Conference of University Professors (NCUP, 1991) set out a summary of standards for the professoriate. These standards may be summarized as follows:

- Established chairs: be of high academic distinction and provide leadership of the subject.
- Personal chairs: be scholars of international, or at least national, distinction and remain committed to promoting research within their university department.
- Academic standing: be an outstanding authority in their field and enhance the reputation of their institution.
- Research and scholarship: maintain individual scholarship and research, encouraging colleagues to engage in original work. Undertake scholarly activities outside the university (e.g. examining external theses, acting as an editor or referee for research journals, reviewing research grant proposals, organization of research conferences, holding office in learned societies).
- Teaching: high-quality teaching practice at both undergraduate and postgraduate level.
- Acquisition of resources: generating resources to underpin scholarly and research activity such as assistantships, fellowships, library support, computing facilities, physical space and consumables through successful application for funding internally and externally.
- Powers of communication: ability to express and defend their views cogently in spoken and written communication.

- Services to the wider university community: service within the university (e.g. via committees, review groups, working parties, and Senate or equivalent).
- Services outside the university: contributions to society beyond the provision of teaching and research, including service on local and national boards, consultancy work for public bodies, and availability to make specialist comment in the media.

The NCUP emphasizes the primacy of scholarly attributes – academic standing, research and scholarship, and teaching – over 'associated or complementary attributes which are increasingly needed from professors nowadays but which ought not overtake the first four as qualifications for appointment' (NCUP, 1991). These associated or complementary attributes include resource acquisition, powers of communication, services to the wider university community and services outside the university.

Others have also offered their own analyses of the achievements and qualities required to be a professor. Taylor *et al.* (2009), for example, offer the following list of required qualities:

- a publication record of international standing;
- grant capture credible to the discipline;
- a recognized programme of research;
- clear leadership;
- completed PhD students;
- indicators of recognition across the discipline, such as editorial boards, research council committee membership and visiting professorships.

Although writing in the context of nursing education, the qualities identified by Taylor and colleagues are relevant to most disciplines, although differences of emphasis may be apparent. The balance between publication and the generation of income through securing research grants may vary. For example, in the applied and natural sciences there are higher expectations in general with respect to income generation in the appointment of professors than in the humanities and social sciences. This is partly connected to the nature of research in the 'hard' sciences, where the cost of cutting edge equipment can be significant. It is also connected to the amount of funding available from governments, charitable bodies and commercial organizations. This tends to favour research into the improvement of public health, for example. Moreover, some researchers and scholars in the humanities and social sciences require relatively little funding in order to carry out research. Philosophers and historians tend to need time to conduct individual research rather than large-scale funding for equipment and the employment of research teams.

Nevertheless, in the modern university, time must be accounted for and professorial faculty are increasingly expected to generate funding that will, in effect, cover the cost of their employment and beyond. This means that candidates for professorships in the humanities and social sciences need to pay more attention to grant capture. It is also, of course, a measure of esteem to be awarded a grant regardless of its purely monetary value. The development of bibliometrics means that there is also now emphasis on demonstrating the impact of research and scholarship through citation counts. This is the most common quantitative measure of impact, despite the difficulties this poses for scholars in specialized areas with fewer peers likely to cite their work. Other measures of impact are also used, such as book sales for scholarly monographs or examples of the way in which academics have influenced practice-based settings.

Among my interviewees and respondents there was a clear sense that grant-getting activity had risen in relative importance in recent years as a key criterion in obtaining a professorship. Having a strong publication record was no longer regarded as sufficient in itself. Candidates needed to show that they could attract funding for their research:

> The criteria have changed, I suspect there is more emphasis on money.
>
> (professor of economics)

The increased emphasis on the generation of research income by professors is related to changes in the way research activity is viewed in universities from an accounting perspective. Indirect costs associated with the use of university equipment are now routinely taken into account in a full economic costing approach. Costs such as the use of university premises, including utilities like electricity, the depreciation of equipment, such as computer hardware, and the buy-out time of individuals from other activities now need to be taken into account. The assumption here is that there is an opportunity cost associated with a faculty member undertaking research, as they might otherwise be undertaking other activities generating value to the institution. The incorporation of such costs in what it means to do research means that proportionately more money must be generated than previously to justify undertaking such research on a 'full' economic basis.

The shift in emphasis to grant getting seems to have affected scholars in the arts, humanities and social sciences most, where conventionally there has been more stress placed on publications. While some academics in these fields regard grant getting as a relatively low priority in terms of their modest need for equipment and resources in order to conduct research, they have been forced to take this requirement more seriously in recent years because of the way in which academic time is calculated. Here, rather than regarding research as something that faculty members do as part of their normal activities, such activity needs to be understood under full economic costing approaches as buy-out time, which justifies such work even if this consists of no more than time to think and write as, say, a philosopher without collecting empirical data.

There is no doubt that research and scholarship is the main basis on which professorial appointments are made. An analysis of published university standards for the promotion of faculty to professorial level (Parker, 2008) indicates that the dominant criterion is research. Here, there are differences of emphasis with other areas of contribution often to the fore in support of an application based principally on research, such as 'research with other excellence taken into account' (28 per cent), being a 'well-rounded researcher' (20 per cent) or being a 'pure researcher' (8 per cent). No institution, according to Parker, provides a route to professorship on the basis of being a 'well-rounded teacher'.

My survey revealed that professors place even more emphasis on the importance of research than their institutions do as the basis for their appointment as professors in practice; 60 per cent of professors considered research and/or scholarship in a discipline or professional field as the sole basis of their appointment. More than a third of respondents (36 per cent) attributed their appointment to a more complex combination of factors, which also included teaching excellence and management and/or service within an institution. There were negligible differences on the basis of gender, although professors appointed in the pure and natural science disciplines were even more likely to cite their research and/or scholarship as the sole reason for their appointment (71 per cent), and were correspondingly less likely to have been made a professor on the basis of a combination of factors including research, teaching and management and/or service (29 per cent). Overall, a mere 2 per cent attributed their professorial title solely to management and/or service within the institution, while less than 1 per cent considered it was due to teaching excellence.

Tacit knowledge

Excellence in teaching tends to play a more significant role in academic promotion at assistant and associate professor levels than at full or chair professor level (Parker, 2008). Parker's survey indicated that no appointments at full professorial level are formally based on being a 'well-rounded teacher'. Also, it is important to understand that while university promotion criteria might indicate formal equality between research and teaching functions, this does not necessarily translate into practice or the perception of practice among professors. There is a body of tacit knowledge or understanding connected with attaining a professorial position, and this includes the perception that, regardless of institutional efforts to reward

Table 5.1 Basis of appointment as a professor (n = 229), %

Research and/or scholarship in a discipline or professional field	60
Management and/or service to the institution	2.0
Teaching excellence	0.9
Combination of these	36

good or excellent teaching, it counts for comparatively little in appointments at professorial level.

Moreover, very few respondents, less than 1 per cent, indicated that teaching and learning was the main basis of their appointment, despite the development of such a specialized route to a professorial position in an increasing number of UK universities. It may be that it is still too early to see the result of such a route, or that there is more rhetoric than action surrounding this possibility. Creating robust criteria of equivalence to research excellence is one of the challenges facing an institution looking to create teaching and learning professors. Criteria with respect to publication outputs for such positions tend to be more broadly framed, and might include the generation of materials used by other university teachers in practice. Research and publication activity here might incorporate action research projects, articles sharing good practice and student textbooks (Hogg, 2007). This contrasts with making an appointment on the basis of a conventional research profile. Such outputs would not normally be regarded as appropriate in indicating someone has reached the level of professor on the basis of their research. Despite efforts to raise the status of a teaching route to professorship, it tends to be regarded 'as a sort of second-class, second-status, not so good pathway' compared with research (Strike, 2010, p. 87).

As a result, there is a clear tension in making appointments on the basis of achievements in learning and teaching and it is doubtful whether appointees will enjoy equivalence of status. The NCUP notes in its 1991 document, outlining the standards required for the professoriate, that while there was wide agreement within the organization about the criteria identified, there was some divergence of opinion with respect to the relative importance of teaching (NCUP, 1991). One of my interviewees, a professor of learning and teaching who had written a large number of student textbooks and managed a discipline-specific national teaching and learning centre, attributed his appointment to something other than research. However, he expressed his discomfort about the unusual nature of his own appointment as a professor, in the context of working in a research-intensive university:

> I am a very unusual professor in this university and feel quite self-conscious about this. The general conversation is about research but I have done minimal research ...
>
> (professor of learning and teaching)

Tacit knowledge further consists of things such as the number of first-authored refereed publications considered as a benchmark for professorial appointments. This kind of information is not contained in university handbooks or guidelines, but exists within the folklore of institutions. Several of the professors I spoke to made the point that they needed to demonstrate a basic level of competence or commitment to roles other than research, such as teaching and administrative duties. However, they were clear that what really counts is research excellence, demonstrated through publication and securing large grants. Being a competent teacher and administrator was expected, but it was really excellence in the field of research that led to a professorship being conferred:

> ... it was entirely down to research, there were even sort of semi-official guidelines in that you should have about 30 good journal papers and you should have been bringing in half a million pounds a year for the past five years, or something. The rules were quite well known ...
>
> (professor of engineering)

> ... I think publications was a major factor [i.e. in being appointed as a professor]. The second factor was research proposals ... we were awarded about a quarter of a million [pounds sterling]. I also had a few PhDs that had gone through the pipeline.
>
> (professor of management)

> ... it is generally understood that to become a reader [a grade just below that of professor in a UK university] you need around 20 refereed papers ...
>
> (professor of history)

Most interviewees argued that research and scholarship ought to be the main basis for appointing professors, and that the criteria should not be broadened in this regard to those whose principal contribution comes from teaching or service to the institution. This view runs counter to the views of those who promote respect for the scholarship of teaching and learning, a movement that draws inspiration from the work of Ernest Boyer (1990). His view was that a broader understanding of four different forms of scholarship (discovery, integration, application and teaching) should be adopted. Boyer's four forms of scholarship have subsequently found their way into the appointment and promotions criteria of many universities, most notably by including recognition for the scholarship of teaching as well as the scholarship of discovery that is associated with research into the discipline. Arguably, however, this has bifurcated teaching and research recognition rather than bringing about an equality of recognition.

Despite recognition among my interviewees of the dominant role of research it was argued that, occasionally, the circumstances affecting a small department might elevate the importance of criteria other than research excellence. This might include appointing someone with a more modest research record who has the potential to be a future head of department. Although research was primary, some interviewees commented that appointment panels expected professors to be able to demonstrate a more all-round set of skills:

> Academic management, teaching, your standing within the teaching community. These things are also now regarded as an important factor. I didn't feel that was necessarily the case a decade ago.
>
> (professor of health science)

Despite recognition that the basis for becoming a professor has broadened to some extent, nearly all interviewees, and the majority of respondents who commented on the issue, were clear that while other criteria might be taken into account, they were not legitimate or sufficient on their own. The possession of an international reputation in a disciplinary or professional field was seen as key to a legitimate professorial level appointment, and some form of publication was regarded as critical for obtaining such a reputation or evidence of impact. Overall, it is clear that despite recent attempts to broaden the basis of promoting university faculty to include a strong emphasis on teaching, practice is largely unchanged.

The survey showed that over 40 per cent of male respondents had at least 11 years' experience in the professorial role compared with only around 17 per cent of women. While the criteria for becoming a professor was not perceived as differing markedly between male and female respondents, slightly more women reported that they occupied faculty or university-wide management roles. Men, on the other hand, are slightly more likely to attribute their appointment as a professor purely on the basis of their research and scholarship compared to women. Hence, as professors, women are more likely to occupy managerial positions of responsibility as opposed to being a professor without a management portfolio. However, male professors are far more likely to hold a management position on a permanent basis (at 52 per cent) compared with women (at just 37 per cent).

In terms of service to the institution, around a third of female professors (31 per cent) reported being asked to serve on university-level committees. This contrasts with just 13.5 per cent of male contemporaries. Men, on the other hand, were more likely than women to be asked to represent the university in an external context. Asked to comment on the relative importance of various roles they might undertake as a professor, all respondents regarded leadership in research with virtually no difference on the basis of gender. Over 88 per cent of women regarded leadership in teaching as either important or very important, compared with 81 per cent of male professors. These figures are consistent with the view that women in higher education still continue to perform a disproportionate amount of academic housework, while male academics are less collegially focused.

Standards and equality issues

There was a perception among most of my interviewees that it had become easier to obtain a professorial position. The growth of new disciplines, such as accountancy, was seen as one of the reasons why becoming a professor might be more easily obtainable. According to a professor in this discipline, appointments to chairs in his field had been 'tainted by the necessity to pay high salaries to get people, and the only way to pay high salaries was to give them the title'. The perception that it is now easier to become a professor was also attributed, in part, to the growth of the UK higher education sector, and the rise in the number of institutions creating a more active transfer market for professors, a situation seen to have been exacerbated by the UK research assessment exercise, which has been operating periodically since 1986.

A professor commented that appointing someone as a 'reader' (a level of appointment found in UK universities in recognition of scholarly achievement only slightly below that of a full professor) can be used as a means of 'avoiding having people poached' (i.e. tempted to leave the university by another institution). A professor of accountancy was told to make the case that he was of professorial quality by obtaining an offer from another university, and was then offered a chair at his existing institution, which he accepted. Illustrating the transfer market, another interviewee mentioned that he was offered a readership in order to stay at a (more prestigious) university, but decided to accept the offer of a professorship at a different, less elite institution:

> I had a difficult decision. Is a reader there better than a professor here? So I took a calculated decision to become a professor and to move.
>
> (professor of management)

The impression that professorial level appointments are now easier to obtain is, to some extent, borne out by the official figures available in the UK. The percentage of academic staff holding a professorial position remained relatively unchanged from the mid 1960s, albeit in an exponentially larger higher education system through to the mid 2000s. In 1964, the percentage of professors at UK universities was 12 per cent, compared with just over 10 per cent in 2008 (Halsey, 1992; HESA, 2009). However, the figures have shown some steady increase, especially over the last few years. In 2004/05, around 9 per cent of UK academic faculty held a professorial position, but by 2009/10 this figure stood at 14.5 per cent (HESA, 2011). The increased proportion may be due to a variety of factors, including a major job evaluation exercise that took place in UK universities in the late 2000s. It is important to note though that the proportion of professors in the UK is still considerably lower than that found in doctoral-granting universities in the United States, where the comparative figure is 35.5 per cent (AAUP, 2011b). Here, a more common expectation is that a professorial position is something that might be obtained before retirement, and it is also closely linked to the tenure system that does not operate in a UK context.

While there has been a feminization of the academy, particularly in the composition of the student population, the proportion of female professors is considerably lower than the number of men holding such positions. Less than one in five professors in the UK is female (HESA, 2011), and the situation in many other European countries is similar. A number of female professors commented that they felt they had faced particular barriers connected with their gender in becoming a professor. Sometimes being held back was attributed to a poor personal relationship with an influential individual, such as a male head of department or a dean:

> ... my then head of department disliked me and I was turned down for a reader twice, even though I fulfilled the criteria ...
>
> (professor of film studies)

Gender issues were specifically cited by three further interviewees as to why it had taken them longer to become a professor than their male counterparts (e.g. 'being a mouthy woman'). Sometimes this was attributed to working in male-dominated subject areas or because of the influence of freemasonry, which was cited by two female professors. Freemasonry is an ancient fraternal organization found in the UK that excludes women from membership.

> I was the first woman professor who had a personal chair in the Faculty of Science. ... I was the first to have a personal chair and I think it is very difficult for women particularly to come to a professorship position, primarily because you are working very much in a male dominated cell, especially in science and engineering, and technology.
>
> (professor of chemical engineering)

> I know of people, indeed probably some in this university, who have been given professorships either because they've got staying power or because they know the right people, or because they are masons.
>
> (professor of film studies)

> ... there is a secret brotherhood up there [i.e. at senior management level].
>
> (professor of applied technology)

Other female interviewees also referred to a lack of transparency about how people become professors, and how this tends to act as a particular barrier to female academics with fewer women role models to guide them. Moreover, it was pointed out that the imbalance in the proportion of male to female professors is not reflected at lower levels within the profession where, for example, a far higher proportion of females often fill post-doctoral positions.

Conclusion

The criteria by which someone becomes a professor are normally well articulated in formal university regulations relating to promotions and appointments. There is now a stronger emphasis internationally on research standing and the measures that offer evidence of the impact of high-quality scholarship, such as citation rates for publications, in addition to the ability of an academic to generate funding. This is an indicator of the creeping influence of 'academic capitalism' (Slaughter and Leslie, 1997, see Chapter 9).

The appointment of professors is intricately associated with the micropolitics of the academy: who likes whom, who is 'in' and who is 'out' of favour and so on.

While published criteria may be freely available, decisions to appoint or not to appoint professors need to be understood in this social and economic context. The appointment of professors is frequently linked to institutional ambitions and used as a tool of management accordingly. The financial health of the institution, personal relationships and attitudes of key figures, notably the vice chancellor, are key to the process.

Hence, the published formal criteria can tell only part of the story. The use of peer review to determine appointments means that there is inevitably a good deal of tacit knowledge that underpins interpretation in practice. This has meant that certain groups, notably women and possibly other under-represented groups, have been historically disadvantaged, remaining for the large part outside the 'loop' of this type of insider knowledge. For the sake of equity and openness it is important that the way professorial appointments are made are as transparent as possible if talent is not to be lost or unfairly held back.

Chapter 6

Being a professor

Introduction

I first became a full professor in 2004 and I distinctly remember preparing, as part of the process, for an interview that would determine whether I would be awarded the title. Prior to this, I had submitted a substantial document detailing my various publications, grants and other achievements. I was interviewed by a small panel who were assembled to determine whether I met the criteria, including the university vice chancellor, the deputy vice chancellor and an external referee. Clearly, the external's opinion would be critical to the eventual decision. As part of my preparations for the interview, I searched around for any literature about what professors are expected to do. I did this because I anticipated being questioned about how I would see my role, and sure enough I was asked about this subsequently in the interview.

However, but for a few exceptions (e.g. Tight, 2002), and despite my best efforts, I found virtually no consideration in the literature about what it means to *be* a professor in the sense of an elaboration of the dispositions, duties, responsibilities and activities they might be expected to undertake. There was plenty of relatively repetitive guidance about how you *become* a professor, as I identified in the previous chapter. Hence, whilst the criteria associated with how to become a professor is relatively clear, what it means to actually *be* one is rarely examined. I remember thinking this was both frustrating and odd. In many ways this experience was the genesis for this book.

I will therefore focus in this chapter on what it means to *be* a professor, and take this discussion on into two further chapters that seek to identify the qualities professors need in order to be intellectual leaders. I will argue that, despite the preferred self-image of most professors as all-rounders, the role of the professor is rapidly fragmenting or unbundling into five types of professor. The 'all-round' or 'classic' professor of the past who taught, researched and often led the department is being replaced by a new generation of specialists in research, practice and management.

The 'bad' professor

In the popular imagination, university professors might appear to fit the caricature of the intellectual sketched out in the first chapter. Shaped and reinforced
by numerous novels, movies, animated games and other fictional representations,
professors are eccentric and unworldly individuals. Generally speaking they do
not tend to get a good press. At best they are shown as eccentric, as in the 1961
movie *The Absent-Minded Professor*, or as sweet but sexually naïve, as in *The Nutty
Professor* (1963, and remade in 1996). In this latter movie, the central character,
Julius Kelp, creates an alter ego, 'Buddy Love', via a laboratory serum that
transforms him into a 'cool' and trendy antithesis of the normally shy and acci-
dent-prone boffin. The notion that professors are intellectuals lacking in any
emotional intelligence is a familiar theme. Possibly the best known example of
this is the character of Professor Henry Higgins in George Bernard Shaw's play
Pygmalion. While a brilliant professor of phonetics, Henry Higgins is insensitive
and manipulative in his treatment of the flower girl, and soon-to-be society belle,
Eliza Doolittle. Sometimes, professors are portrayed as more misguided, evil or
sinister characters like Professor Moriarty, Sherlock Holmes' arch-enemy in the
novels of Arthur Conan Doyle. It is rare for a professor to be portrayed as a hero.
The Indiana Jones movie series is an exception that proves the point.

So, on the whole, the image of the professor is not exactly a positive one.
They are seen as intellectuals with the qualities and flaws associated with this
caricature: unworldly, vain and malleable. The various epithets about professors outlined by Logan Wilson in his classic account of academic life, *The
Academic Man*, are just as fixed in the popular imagination today as they were
back in 1942 when the book was published. They are fed by the continuing,
often negative, and mainly gendered, cultural representations of professors down
the ages:

> Some representative epithets (for professors) were: lacking breadth, monkish,
> dull, funny little fellows, absent-minded and bigoted, sheepish, stultified,
> garrulous, queer, lacking virility, fugitives from reality, absurdly theoretical,
> lacking conviction, unimaginative, oracular, tradition bound, and lazy.
>
> (Wilson, 1942, p. 151)

But it would be a mistake to dismiss such criticisms as groundless. The position
enjoyed by universities, especially elite public universities, is still a comparatively
privileged one and open to abuse. Echoes of Wilson's list of epithets can be
found in a characterization of how some professors are perceived in an essay by
Susan Bassnett (2004, p. 3):

> Idle, unwilling to support younger colleagues, content to let the burden
> of undergraduate teaching fall on other shoulders, distant, authoritarian.
> So-called research professors were the most despised.

This quotation contains a worrying list of accusations connected, to some extent, to the competitive ethos of modern university life. Normally such activity is for the benefit of the institution, or more directly for a research project or team of individuals. However, sometimes income generation is also about consultancy work for personal gain. Professors in a business school, whose primary goal is to create as many money-making opportunities as possible through consultancy work, have been labelled 'cowboys' (Piercy, 1999). This professorial stereotype is also said to perform poorly in terms of publications, and can resort to various tactics to give the appearance of research activity, including buying joint authorship on papers or becoming a 'data vulture' who preys on young and impressionable researchers in order to persuade them to cede unwarranted authorship credit for minimal effort (Piercy, 1999). While this might be a caricature, it is important not to dismiss such criticisms lightly as this represents a recognized form of behaviour. Sadly some professors do fit the stereotype. One of my respondents made the following characterization of the 'worst-case scenario' professor:

> ... a mediocre researcher (with little credibility among academic staff) who is also a poor or careless teacher (lack of interest in student development is symptomatic of poor mentoring and leadership skills), and an unreliable or incompetent administrator who hides his/her deficiencies in scholarship or teaching ability behind his/her administrative role; a manager who is inflexible, pessimistic and passive in outlook (looking backwards full of nostalgia rather than forwards in terms of current and future challenges and how to meet them constructively); an individual who is either too weak to establish or maintain fair working conditions or deliberately operates a system of nepotism (towards those considered non-challenging) and harassment (towards junior colleagues with enormous potential). Such a leader will insist on time-serving and will deliberately block early promotion or overload individuals to delay promotion, and/or will exploit the ideas and work of junior colleagues for his/her own research. Unfortunately this is not an imaginary scenario. I know of many such cases in the UK and elsewhere.
>
> (questionnaire respondent)

Some characteristics of 'bad professors' that were identified by my own respondents and interviewees included an inclination to nepotism, a lack of interest in teaching or the development of students and conveying overly negative or pessimistic attitudes about working conditions. Harassing or bullying junior colleagues was also cited. The motivation for this latter form of behaviour was explained in terms of either trying to damage the confidence of those who might be perceived as a threat in terms of their academic potential, or exploiting their intellectual ideas without giving authorship credit. A more general criticism of professors is that they are selfish and unwilling to contribute to activities that do not fall squarely within their relatively specialized area of interest:

Heads of departments will talk about one of the most difficult things they have is professors who refuse to do their share of the work, who throw their weight around, those sorts of things, so of course from the point of view of being a manager, professors can insist that they are listened to and can be a damn nuisance.

(professor of engineering and head of department)

There are an awful lot of professors who really don't want to do any leadership and management things and want to tick over. I do think, at the very least, you would expect serious research guidance, mentoring and genuine collaboration on papers and grants with other members of staff as a minimal expectation of a professor.

(professor of economics and head of department)

The 'worst-case scenario' professor is a reality, although fortunately individuals do not always combine all the faults detailed in such a characterization. Abuse of power is a risk among senior members of any profession, no less so among professors. This can occur in an academic context where the ideas of others are exploited without adequate acknowledgement. Here, doctoral students as well as junior faculty members are often the ones to fall victim, accepting such practices as normal or something they feel unable to object given the power imbalance in the relationship. Authorial credit is a key area of common abuse. While universities have invested considerable efforts in recent years to improve research ethics, this tends to be limited to the protection of human subjects. Too rarely do they explicitly address authorship issues.

Mismatched expectations

However, as in any walk of life, there will always be unscrupulous individuals who fail to appreciate that leadership is a privilege rather than a right. Most professors though are anxious to ensure that they live up to the expectations that the position brings. They want to do a good job, but while universities publish guidelines about how someone might *become* a professor, institutions pay comparatively little attention to what professors are expected to *do*. At its simplest, this might be expressed as to profess their subject, but this somewhat anodyne phrase fails to capture the richness of the role of a professor. My survey of university professors asked respondents to comment on how they saw their role, and also to what extent their views correspond with their university's expectations of them (Macfarlane, 2011a). This was partly based on a list of nine roles related to the work of a professor adapted from the work of Tight (2002).

I asked respondents to consider the relative importance of these roles (see Table 6.1). The results indicated that 'helping other colleagues to develop' was rated as the most important, followed closely by 'leadership in research', 'being a

Table 6.1 The role of a professor (rated important or very important) by rank order

Helping other colleagues to develop	100
Leadership in research	98
Being a role model	98
Upholding standards of scholarship	96
Influencing the work and direction of the university	88
Influencing public debate	84
Leadership in teaching	84
Representing the department in the university	76
Income generation	49

role model' and 'upholding the standards of scholarship'. There were very high levels of agreement with the importance of all these roles. By contrast, 'income generation' was regarded as the least important of the nine roles, with just under half of respondents rating it as either important or very important.

Respondents were further asked to comment on what they perceived to be the expectations of their university institutions with respect to their role as opposed to their own personal ideal. This produced an alternate rank order of roles (see Table 6.2) with some notable differences. For example, professors ranked income generation activities as their least important role but considered that it was second only to leadership in research as an institutional expectation. This is a significant mismatch in expectations between how professors see their role and what they believe their institutions are looking for.

Another difference of note was that respondents felt their own institutions were far less interested in their contributions to local activities by contrast to their own preferences in this respect. Professors perceived 'influencing the work and direction of the university' and 'representing the department in the university' as the two roles their universities least valued. This reinforces the sense of exclusion from university management, leadership and decision-making processes that some professors talked to me about.

Table 6.2 The expectations of universities (rated important or very important) by rank order

Leadership in research	91
Income generation	78
Upholding standards of scholarship	66
Helping other colleagues to develop	64
Being a role model	60
Influencing public debate	61
Leadership in teaching	61
Influencing the work and direction of the university	55
Representing the department in the university	49

Formal leadership roles

Many professors do occupy formal managerial positions. These typically include being a head of department or a dean of a wider grouping of departments, normally referred to as a faculty or school. Professors may also be heads of research centres, taught and doctoral programmes, and significant university committees (e.g. research ethics). University-wide leadership roles occupied by professors tend to be senior positions, such as director of the institution's graduate school, vice president (or pro-vice chancellor) or president (or vice chancellor). I found that professors in English post-1992 universities are more than twice as likely to hold a university-wide managerial role, compared with their counterparts in pre-1992 institutions. While 17 per cent of professors held such posts in post-1992 institutions, the figure for pre-1992s was a mere 6 per cent. However, more respondents from pre-1992 universities (38 per cent) held faculty-based management roles than those from the post-1992 universities (25 per cent) (Macfarlane, 2011a). It is also more likely that professors in older, pre-1992 UK universities will occupy formally designated research leadership positions, while a higher proportion of their counterparts at newer, post-1992 universities will be expected to offer leadership contributions in respect to teaching and administration.

However, only a tiny proportion (around 2 per cent) indicated that this management role was the main basis for their appointment (see Chapter 5). Once appointed as a professor, though, many are expected to undertake, or to continue to serve, in some managerial capacity. While this is sometimes seen as administrative support staff undertaking work previously the domain of academics, it is also about academics undertaking more professional support work as an integrated part of their shifting identity. More often than not undertaking a hybrid role was seen as a struggle, and sometimes even dysfunctional. Just two of my respondents, both from post-1992 universities, commented that their management role was indistinguishable from their professorial role. Most professors, therefore, see the roles of professor and manager as distinct.

Yet while a dual or multi-identity is a growing phenomenon in higher education as work becomes more 'blended' between academic and professional domains (Whitchurch, 2006), the trend is in the opposite direction for professors. Over two-fifths of professors (44 per cent) occupy hybrid roles on either a faculty or university-wide basis. In other words they are *both* a professor and a manager. But occupying a dual role in this way was considerably more common in a past age when the role of professor and head of department was practically indistinguishable. While it is relatively common for professors to have blended identities in hybridized roles, the majority of respondents in my survey do not hold a formal managerial position. Here there is a contrast with earlier times when academic departments might have had just one professor, and this individual would have been expected as a matter of course to fulfill the role of head of department (see Chapter 3). Hence, there was not such a stark division between being a professor and being an academic leader as the one more or less implied the other. Clearly, though, professors without formal institutional management positions still undertake leadership roles externally in the context of their discipline or profession by working, for example, as journal editors, leaders of scholarly societies and associations or in positions of responsibility for professional accrediting bodies, external examination boards or research councils.

Professors frequently feel torn about playing a formal management or leadership role. Most feel it is part of their duty as a professor, but they are also very conscious that unless they are looking to develop a managerial career, it can have adverse consequences for their own scholarship:

> It [i.e. being a manager] screws your career. I mean as head of department you've completely wiped out two or three years, you may have lost your ideas, you've certainly lost your role, lost your place in the research ratings.
>
> (professor of film studies)

Others were clearer that departmental leadership is not a role for a professor. This was largely based on seeing the professorial role from a research-based perspective:

> I don't think professors should run the department, because then they will never do the things they are supposed to do which is research and intellectual leadership.
>
> (professor of management)

Locals and cosmopolitans

Respondents were asked to consider the ways in which their institution drew on their expertise. Working as a research leader and a mentor to inexperienced colleagues were the most highly ranked, while just one-third of respondents indicated that they had been asked to advise senior managers on specialist subjects (see Table 6.3). Notably, three-fifths of respondents (61 per cent) felt their expertise was either used 'a little' or 'not at all'.

Table 6.3 The ways institutions use professorial expertise (rated important or very important) by rank order

Leading research or innovation projects and groups	79
Mentoring inexperienced researchers and teachers	75
Serving on university committees	62
Developing external links	58
Representing the university in an external context	54
Advising senior managers on specialist subjects	33

Comments within this section of the questionnaire expressed a general view that use of expertise within a local context takes place without much recognition or explicit encouragement. Typical anonymous comments include:

> Whilst I engage in many of these activities, this is not institution driven and frankly they probably have no idea what I am doing.

> I do mentor, but this is not sponsored by the institution. I do it because I see it as a moral obligation of the role, and because people welcome it when offered. Others approach and ask for it.
>
> (questionnaire respondents)

In a similar vein, one respondent commented that considerably more use of their expertise is made as a visiting professor to another institution rather than their primary employing university. Here, there was a clear sense that professors felt excluded from the local context. They were seen as individuals who could win external funding and publish in international journals, rather than contribute significantly within the university to local activities. Hence, their professional identity and reputation was regarded as existing principally beyond the walls of the institution.

This perception invokes the well-established distinction made by Merton (1947) between locals and cosmopolitans in respect to roles within communities. This distinction was subsequently developed further by Gouldner (1957) in relation to membership of formal organizations. According to Merton, cosmopolitans have a high base of professional skill or expertise, and identify most strongly with an outer reference group rather than members of the immediate organization. They are also low on loyalty to the organization. By contrast, locals have less commitment to specialized role skills, but are highly loyal to their employing organization, and identify principally to an inner reference group found within the organization. Gouldner applied this distinction to faculty at a US liberal arts college, finding differences that reflected it in relation to academic life. Cosmopolitans were likely to place more emphasis on their research priorities, published more, got their intellectual stimulation from outside the college, were more willing to leave for another institution and tended to know fewer people within the institution than locals. A more recent exploration of tenure-tracked academics has identified a similarly relevant distinction between careers that are boundaried and those that are boundaryless (Dowd and Kaplan, 2005).

Perceptions among professors that they are often excluded from the 'local' context include their (limited) role in university governance. Here, there was a strong sense, especially among professors in post-1992 universities, that they were unfairly excluded from decision making at a senior level. This was expressed most strongly by a professor who had formerly worked in a pre-1992 university and was now working in a post-1992 institution:

> Professors and readers should automatically be on any executive body which makes far-reaching decisions about how an academic institution

functions ... [otherwise] it is like having a commercial enterprise, where you have managing directors and a board of directors and all the decisions are made by the second tier management.

(professor of oncology)

Some professors went further, and commented that not only did they feel their views were unwanted but that, if they expressed them, they ran the risk of being ostracized in the context of a 'macho' management culture:

Unless you trot out the party line you would be foolish to speak out. If you speak up it can affect your career progression.

(professor of marketing)

In many respects the characteristics of cosmopolitans reflect the popular image of the professor. They are individuals who are perceived as both research-focused and more likely to identify with professional colleagues outside the institution. *In extremis*, this can lead to professors being characterized in the sort of negative terms discussed at the beginning of the chapter as, for example, 'cowboys' (Piercy, 1999, p. 698) selfishly pursuing paid consultancy interests while contributing comparatively little to teaching or service activities within the faculty. This is about a lack of responsibility for the internal life of the institution and has been encouraged by research audit exercises in places such as the UK, Hong Kong, New Zealand and Australia. It creates a pressure internationally for scholars to conform to research productivity expectations, and means that cosmopolitanism has come to define the reward and recognition of the university professor at the expense of the local role (Altbach 2006).

Unbundling

Therefore, what it means to be a professor has shifted over the last 20 or 30 years. Before the global expansion of higher education there were comparatively few universities and, hence, relatively fewer professors. Those who attained a professorial position were often expected to take on a role as a head of department, since this was essential to ensure that these collective interests were represented at the university level via the senate, to which full professors belonged. However, the situation now is quite different in many ways. University governance has been corporatized, and the role of the professoriate, and other academic faculty, diminished in terms of power and decision-making influence (Harloe and Perry, 2005).

Many of my interviewees expressed a frustration that they played a limited and often isolated role in the university. At the same time, the demands on departments, to demonstrate efficiency and value for money in a competitive environment, means that the administrative burdens of departmental leadership have also increased beyond those formerly associated with professors as intellectual leaders. Critically, though, the role of research is much greater in the modern university via international performance indicators both individually (e.g. citation rates) and institutionally (world rankings of universities). This means that professors are now largely seen mainly as specialists in research, rather than broader aspects of the academic role as part of the unbundling of academic life. In many areas, there has been a significant increase in funding opportunities for modern academic researchers, with the growth of national research councils and charities with interests especially focused on health (Grant and Drakich, 2010).

The word academic tends to be associated with someone who teaches, researches and also performs a variety of service roles such as serving on university committees or undertaking administrative tasks including leading others (Kogan *et al.*, 1994). It is a common presumption that being a so-called all-round academic is the norm. Yet this situation is changing quite rapidly, and this conventional understanding of academic life is out of kilter with a new, emerging reality. In truth, fewer and fewer faculty can be classified as all-round academics. Universities are diversifying their career pathways and the range of recognized academic roles and titles. In a British context this diversity includes 'teaching and research assistants and fellows, research- or teaching-only faculty, academic administrators, learning and teaching coordinators, academic consultants, enterprise fellows, directors of research, and directors of education alongside the more traditional professor' (Strike, 2010, p. 91). In 2008–09, just 51.7 per cent of those employed on academic contracts had a teaching and research function in the UK (HESA, 2011). In the US, over half of full-time appointments of new academic staff in the 1990s were to non-tenured and fixed-term contracts (Finkelstein and Schuster, 2001). These figures indicate that the academic profession is disaggregating into specialized roles and parallel pathways for teachers and researchers (Macfarlane, 2011c).

Universities now rely even very heavily on non-professorial faculty to teach. This has always occurred, to some extent, but has been exacerbated by the trend toward research intensity and technological advances. Academic functions are being subcontracted to a growing army of para-academics: individuals who specialize in one element of academic life. A plethora of para-academic roles now exist connected with this devolution of responsibilities (Coaldrake, 2001). Para-academics perform specialist functions in relation to either teaching, research or service, and also include doctoral students with teaching responsibilities and faculty employed on a part-time, portfolio (Brown and Gold, 2007) or casual basis. Here it is important to emphasize that being a para-academic is not exclusively connected to professional support roles. Para-academics are being created via research specialization among (full) professors and the creation of managerial career tracks. While there is clearly a difference in academic prestige between, for example, a learning technologist and a research professor, they are both specialist professionals rather than all-rounders.

Academics whose scholarship is deemed insufficiently robust or are failing to publish enough may find themselves appointed to teaching-only contracts. This pattern of disaggregation is occurring in relation to the research role as the university employs specialist research grant-getting and management staff, designed to increase the success and productivity of faculty. This is the environment that has produced research professors who have no teaching responsibilities or administrative responsibilities (see later in this chapter). In regard to the service or administrative role, there is now an array of para-academics supporting students and staff such as dyslexia advisors, faculty developers and student counselors.

One of the problems with unbundling is that while roles may be redefined on a formal basis, the professional identity of the individual affected is less easily changed. This results in a divergence between the *identity* of many of those working in higher education and their *role*. The identity of a teaching-only appointee is likely to be steeped in the conventions of their discipline with an interest or some expertise, at least in part, for knowledge production and communication. However, the formal contract of this individual excludes this activity. It is widely acknowledged that the centre of academic life is the discipline (Henkel, 2000). This includes producing new knowledge as a researcher and teaching based on cognate expertise.

The academic role has been narrowed in practice by a range of system-wide forces, leading to a diminution of their teaching and administrative functions. Others with academic identities have seen their research role wither as they are driven into specialist functions as teachers or managers. There is growing usage of the term para-academic in university parlance, and it may be found especially in Canadian and US institutions, where it is employed to refer mainly to administrative units associated with the enhancement of learning and teaching processes, such as centres for faculty or academic development.

The limited extent to which the term para-academic is used and applied in university organizations belies the increasing specialization of academic roles. The usage tends to apply to a limited number of staff who may be referred to as *de jure* para-academics, those whose formal job description reflects the reality of their role as a specialist in one aspect of academic practice such as a learning technologist. Others are essentially *de facto* para-academics who, while formally employed as an all-round academic, effectively focus on just one element of academic practice. An example of a *de facto* para-academic is a lecturer who, while formally employed to conduct teaching, research and service, is research inactive and performs very few service functions, relying instead on referral to other para-academics (for example, specialist personal tutors, educational developers, careers advisers). This type of academic is, in effect, simply a teacher. Similarly, many academics who are appointed to managerial roles relinquish teaching and research work as a result, becoming *de facto* para-academics, but retain an academic contract of employment for 'teaching and research' connected with pension provision. They are in practice simply managers. This scenario applies especially to those who are appointed to permanent rather than rotating managerial roles as, for example, a head of department or dean of faculty, and to a number of other more senior management positions: a pattern most commonly found in post-1992 English universities.

Changing identities

The disaggregation of the academic profession is resulting in new labels for classifying academics within institutions, often on the basis of their orientation toward teaching, research, entrepreneurship or leadership and management. Apart from the 'classic academic' who teaches, does some research and performs service tasks in roughly equal proportions, there is now a splintering, in practice, into a wider variety of roles such as 'entrepreneurial researcher', the 'engaged academic' and the 'disciplinary research leader' (Coates and Goedegebuure, 2010).

These changes mean that there are now many different types of professor, just as there are many different types of academic. The *classic professor* is one who researches, teaches and leads often in the role of head of department. This model dates from when there were fewer professors and probably only one per academic department, making the discharge of managerial responsibilities a necessity. It also relates to a time when academic life was less dominated by research and publication, and the interests of academics were more diverse and teaching-led (Halsey and Trow, 1971; Wilson, 1979). The reinvention of the university as a research-intensive organization over the last 20 years has shifted the role of the professor away from being an all-rounder. Parker's (2008) research found that the category of 'all-rounder with a specialism' represented just 14 per cent of 'routes' to professorship.

This means that the classic or all-round professor is a dying breed. The *research professor* is fast replacing the classic professor as the 'traditional' model stimulated by national audit exercises of research excellence in the UK, Australia and elsewhere, together with an expanding transfer market for researchers with strong international profiles and the capacity to generate funding and high citation rates. Indeed, the phrase research professor is now in common usage throughout the world, to distinguish the role of someone holding such a chair from others where expectations to perform teaching and service tasks are greater. One of my anonymous survey respondents made the following comment explaining the shift from the classic to the research professor role:

> I think there was an older model of the professorial role, which naturally assumed you would be active in research, a knowledgeable and inspiring teacher, a role model to colleagues, engaged with the larger community, and a shrewd and efficient administrator. That model is now defunct, to judge by most appointments in my field. There is now more specialization in the professorial role, and above all, a professor must be seen to be research active right to the end of their careers – quite a tall order for many.
>
> (questionnaire respondent)

Star professors may be identified as high-performing research professors, often headhunted by institutions looking to boost their research reputation or ranking. Those holding established rather than personal chairs (see Chapter 4) are more likely to be considered as 'star professors' due to the comparative scarcity and difficulty in obtaining such a position. Regius professors at some of the ancient British universities would also certainly fit into this category, as they represent possibly the most sought-after positions in a UK context. Star professors have also been created through prestigious national schemes established in a range of countries, including Canada, France, South Africa, Australia and New Zealand, designed to stem the outflow of research talent. The Canada Research Chairs (CRC) programme, launched in 2000 with $900 million of federal funding, is one such example designed to create 2,000 research chairs in Canadian universities (Grant and Drakich, 2010). Another is the Future Fellowships scheme created by the Australian government in 2008 to promote research in areas considered critical in terms of national importance, and to attract as well as stem the loss of talented researchers. Globalization means that the internationalization of academic staff has become more widespread, and star professors are the most mobile on the basis of their research output, grant-getting ability and scholarly reputations.

In addition there are, at least, two further types of professor. The *practice professor* is someone from an applied discipline or profession such as medicine, dentistry, law, architecture or possibly a business or commercial field such as journalism, who is still principally based in this setting. They tend to have a more significant role as a teacher rather than necessarily a researcher, and their more limited contact with the university as an administrative entity means that they normally will do less institutional service than say a classic professor or possibly a research professor. Finally, there is the *managerial professor*. This person holds a formal role as a departmental, faculty or institutional leader. Universities increasingly appoint role holders such as heads of department, deans and members of the senior university management team (e.g. vice chancellor or president; vice

Table 6.4 The unbundled professor

Classic professor	The 'all-round' professor who teaches, researches and performs significant institutional leadership often in the form of a permanent or rotating head of department. A model in decline.
Research professor	A successful researcher with a significant publication and/or track record in acquiring funding. Some teaching and service responsibilities but not seen as core to role. Fast becoming the default model.
Star professor	A leading research professor often headhunted by ambitious or world-leading institutions seeking to enhance or maintain reputation and status. Will normally expect to have little teaching or institutional service responsibility.
Practice professor	Mainly associated with professors in practice fields (e.g. medicine, dentistry, architecture, business, journalism) where role includes significant teaching in applied settings.
Managerial professor	Senior academic leader such as dean of faculty or university-wide leader (e.g. president/vice chancellor, vice president/pro vice chancellor). Unlikely still to be research active or teaching but retaining professorial title.

presidents or pro vice chancellors) on a permanent or contractual basis for terms of office of at least three or five years. Their time is taken up with managerial and other leadership duties that tend to preclude the continuation of any significant research or teaching, although there are exceptional individuals who manage to maintain the role of classic professor. The five roles outlined above are summarized in Table 6.4.

Conclusion

The specialization of the professoriate is a consequence of the massification of higher education and the increasing emphasis on research output and income generation. This is leading to a hollowing out of what it means to be a professor, with many now seeing their role as specialists in research, and more occasionally management or teaching. The majority of my interviewees and respondents though still see the role of a professor in the *classic* mode as someone with all-round expertise and a preparedness to contribute on this basis. While this may be the self-image, the reality is fast changing and it potentially puts at risk the commitment of modern professors to academic leadership within the institution. A cadre of managerial positions is emerging who sometimes, at a relatively early stage in their academic career, decide to focus their energies toward the pursuit of institutional leadership.

A lot of professors, particularly those without a formal leadership or management position, feel a sense of exclusion, disconnection and sometimes isolation within the university. This is partly due to the specialized roles into which they must now fit. This sense of disconnection means that it is vitally important to look at ways in which the leadership role of the professoriate can be redefined and given fresh meaning. The two chapters that follow will begin the process of (re)defining the role of the professoriate as intellectual leaders by examining how they need to balance activities and develop qualities associated with academic freedom and academic duty.

Chapter 7

Two freedoms

Introduction

This chapter, and the next, will consider two different dimensions which contribute to the making of an intellectual leader in higher education. In addressing this matter, these two chapters will identify a number of characteristics or traits, and divide these into ones associated with academic freedom and ones associated mainly with academic duty. My argument here is that a professor as an intellectual leader needs to possess a balance of traits or dispositions associated with both academic freedom and academic duty. In this chapter I will outline the importance of two characteristics associated with academic freedom, which I will argue are essential for intellectual leadership: being a *critic* and being an *advocate*.

These traits come together through seeking to transgress conventional boundaries, principally between disciplines and between academic and public life. This is not just about making a mark. This is about developing ideas, or promoting a way in which to understand the world, which makes a difference to peoples' lives in terms of their physical, social or economic wellbeing. The capacity to offer intellectual leadership is first dependent on the possession of qualities that might normally be associated with being an intellectual. These qualities are about exercising freedoms, but they are only one part of the equation that makes an intellectual leader. This requires the performance of duties (see Chapter 8) as well as the exercise of personal freedoms. The relationship between academic freedom and academic duty is critical to understanding the meaning of intellectual leadership in the university. They inter-relate and depend on each other.

Academic freedom

Academic freedom and academic duty are two sides of the same coin (Kennedy, 1997). One is a necessary corollary of the other. It is an academic duty to protect academic freedom and similarly academic freedom depends on academic duty. The former point may be illustrated by reference to the governance of academic institutions. It is the academic duty of academics at a minimum to participate in the election of their peers to represent the interests of the academic community within university affairs. Here, I am drawing a parallel with the basis for citizenship or participation in any society where one would expect individuals to engage in democratic processes designed to govern that society.

More courage or engagement is required to protect other freedoms, notably freedom of speech. If someone is prevented from exercising their freedom of speech or punished for doing so within the context of their role as an academic, it is the duty of other academics to speak up in protest. Academic freedom also depends on academic duty. It is not possible without it. This point may be exemplified by reference to the peer review process by which papers for publication are read and critiqued by fellow academics. Without this process, and the willingness of academics to give their time and energy in the service of their peers and the development of their discipline, the system by which academics communicate their research would collapse. This is why performative pressures on academics to become more narrowly individualistic are threatening the balance between academic freedom and academic duty, by eroding communal processes such as peer review.

Academic freedom is perhaps *the* cornerstone concept of academic identity. A voluminous literature has evolved devoted to the discussion and elaboration of the meaning of academic freedom. This is about the freedom of thought and expression essential to creativity and criticism. It concerns freedom from fear of retribution and means, among other things, that a university professor should not lose his or her job (or suffer any punishment) simply by expressing views that may conflict with the opinion of the influential or powerful. It is, to use a phrase often attributed to Said (1994), about speaking truth to power. Whether the extent of this freedom of expression should extend outside of a professor's cognate area of expertise is a moot point, with some holding that it should be limited to their area of professional competence (e.g. Karran, 2009; Johnson, 1988). The right to so-called 'extramural utterance and action' beyond the boundaries of someone's discipline was asserted by the American Association for University Professors in 1915 (AAUP, 1915, p. 292) (see Chapter 9). This provides a basis for the claim that a university professor has a legitimate right to address a subject in a public forum outside of his or her discipline or scholarly field. However, the right to extramural freedom remains contested.

The basic rationale for academic freedom is that it ensures universities can provide government and wider society with dispassionate advice. Such a freedom from interference ultimately better serves the interests of the nation-state. This was von Humboldt's argument on the founding of the University of Berlin in 1836, and is a bedrock principle that has underpinned the subsequent spread of the Humboldtian model of higher education, most notably in the US. Quite simply, if you want to maximize the potential benefits from people with knowledge and ideas, you develop a safe environment, which is conducive to them being able to argue, experiment and think freely. This is what a university is about.

Academic freedom is all too often presented as a self-regarding concept, inasmuch as most definitions are premised on the idea that members of academic faculty are entitled to freedom to teach, to enquire and to offer their opinions about and beyond their discipline. While academic freedom is extended to students in the Germanic tradition via the principle of *Lernfreiheit*, or freedom to learn, this is rarely noted in the literature. In a glaring omission of this dimension, Conrad Russell's book *Academic Freedom* (Russell, 1993) contains no mention of students whatsoever. In the UK, this self-regarding version of academic freedom was reinforced by the protection given to academics, not students, by the Education Reform Act (1988), which states that the jobs of faculty must not be jeopardized by them putting 'forward new ideas and controversial and unpopular opinions' (Section 202[2]).

Universities have conventionally been seen as beacons of free thinking and criticism of the *status quo*, especially in countries where democratic values are absent, weakly established or under threat. However, academic freedom is rarely out of the headlines in countries where democratic values are seen as most strongly established. In the United States and the UK, professional associations and lobby groups such as the American Association of University Professors (AAUP), Scholars at Risk, Academics for Academic Freedom (AFAF) and the Council for Academic Freedom and Academic Standards (CAFAS) further focus attention on cases where academic faculty perceive their freedom to have been undermined.

Threats to academic freedom can take more subtle or insidious forms than simply being punished or prevented from speaking out. Universities acting in a more corporate manner are criticized as restricting the dissemination of academic knowledge through their growing interest in protecting intellectual property rights and doing deals with funders that prevent the publication of market-sensitive scientific research. The limited opportunities that academics have to participate in modern forms of institutional governance, especially, but not exclusively, in post-1992 UK universities, is another more insidious break on academic freedom. The proportion of tenured academic faculty (or those on permanent as opposed to short-term contracts elsewhere) has declined significantly in many national contexts over the last 40 years. In the United States, tenured positions now represent only around one-third of the academic profession having fallen from two-thirds in the mid 1970s (Nelson, 2010). Arguably, this shift in employment patterns has had an effect on the likelihood of academics speaking out on issues such as the management of their own institution, fearing that interventions of this nature might jeopardize their chances of gaining tenure or having a contract renewed. This fear can have an insidious effect, resulting in self-censorship or 'self-intimidation' (Horowitz, 1963). Moreover, the global expansion of higher education means that there are now universities in countries with little history of democratic conventions. In such environments, it is dubious whether academics possess academic freedom in the German tradition.

Professor as critic

Over time our collective understanding about the world changes. This is brought about by sometimes rapid but often gradual 'paradigm shifts'. This phrase was coined by Thomas Kuhn (1962) to refer to the displacement of one conceptual view of the world with another. The work of Charles Darwin changed the way in which people understood the process of evolution. John Maynard Keynes changed the way that economic problems such as unemployment were understood and tackled by governments. Similarly, cognitive psychologists, such as Wilhelm Wundt and Jean Piaget, successfully challenged the idea that psychology could only be studied scientifically through a process of observation. Karl Marx had a fundamental impact on the way people viewed capitalism. He offered a new paradigm based on the shared ownership of production. In more recent times, arguments about the extent to which human activities have been responsible for changing world weather patterns has underpinned the debate about climate change. A new paradigm appears to have emerged, which has, in turn, been critiqued by those unconvinced of its veracity.

Few academics bring about paradigm shifts, but many develop positions that are critical of prevailing theories or beliefs. They follow others in making their own, perhaps minor contribution, to critiquing a popular theory, concept or set of assumptions about the world. Figures associated with major paradigm shifts often rely on or cite others who came before them who were perhaps less influential but, in their view, theoretically 'correct'. For example, the highly influential *General Theory* of Keynes in the field of economics cites the influence of J.A. Hobson, who had previously critiqued the dominance of Say's Law in the way market behaviour was understood within economies.

To be an intellectual leader it is not necessary to bring about a paradigm shift, but it is necessary to develop ideas, concepts, theories or models that are, to some extent, new or novel. This necessitates a degree of engagement with and subsequent criticism of what has come before. This should not be seen simply as negative or destructive in nature, but as the questioning of received wisdom and the interrogation of empirical evidence or the conceptually taken for granted. Indeed, this characteristic is, perhaps more fundamentally, the essence of what it means to possess a 'higher' education (Barnett, 1990). It is what many (if not most) university educators would claim to be doing in helping students to think for themselves and look critically at theoretical and professional knowledge.

Sometimes individuals are strongly associated with the role of critic. Richard Dawkins, former Professor for the Public Understanding of Science at the University of Oxford, is a well-known critic of creationism and the role of religion in society. Dawkins has written a number of influential books such as *The Selfish Gene* (Dawkins, 1976) and more recently *The God Delusion* (Dawkins, 2006), a bestseller that contends there is strong evidence contradicting the existence of a personal god. One of the criticisms levelled at Dawkins is that he writes about a subject (i.e. religion) that lies outside his area of immediate expertise as a professor of evolutionary biology (see Chapter 2). This is the view, for example, of the leading literary critic Terry Eagleton, who opens his review of *The God Delusion* with the following acerbic remark:

> Imagine someone holding forth on biology whose only knowledge of the subject is the *Book of British Birds*, and you have a rough idea of what it feels like to read Richard Dawkins on theology.
>
> (Eagleton, 2006, p. 32)

Regardless of whether one agrees or disagrees with Dawkins' criticism of religious belief, the fundamental argument here, in terms of intellectual leadership, is whether someone can have legitimacy as a critic if their primary discipline does not match the subject on which they are writing. There is a close connection between evolutionary biology and arguments concerning the role of god as a creator of the universe, which have existed since the publication of Darwin's *On the Origin of Species* in the nineteenth century. The counter-criticism levelled at Dawkins though is representative of the modern conception of the university professor as a discipline-based specialist, rather than someone with a legitimate role as a public commentator and critic.

Few modern professors see their role as Dawkins does in extending beyond his immediate specialism into areas of public policy and debate. This is the role of the public intellectual (see Chapter 9). We live in a multiversity rather than a university, with not one but a series of hermetically sealed communities based on specialist research interests:

> It is not one entity but several – the community of the undergraduate and the community of the graduate; the community of the humanist, the community of the social scientist, and the community of the scientist; the communities of the professional schools; the community of the non-academic personnel; the community of the administrators.
>
> (Kerr, 2008, p. 50)

This is the 'reality of separateness' (Bloom, 1987, p. 349) between the humanities and the sciences that, according to Alan Bloom (1987), has existed, at least to some extent, since Kant: someone able to command a significant knowledge and influence as both a natural scientist and a philosopher. Albert Einstein was not just a famous physicist but also contributed ideas on the history and philosophy of science. Modern professors though are specialists rather than renaissance polymaths, who possess knowledge across many areas of science, arts and the humanities. Thus, the fragmentation of disciplinary knowledge in the modern age means it is increasingly problematic for a professor to claim legitimacy as a critic in anything other than his or her own immediate specialism:

> Most university professors are specialists, concerned only with their own fields, interested in the advancement of those fields in their own terms, or in

their own personal advancement in a world where all the rewards are on the side of professional distinction.

(Bloom, 1987, p. 339)

Criticism is also represented in academic life through scholarly movements, such as feminist scholarship, that challenge existing disciplinary fields. In the nineteenth and much of the twentieth century, considerable attention was focused on equal political rights for women. The second wave of feminist activism and scholarship has focused on addressing social and cultural inequalities rather than political rights for women. Feminist scholars from this era finished their graduate education in the mid to late 1960s and sought to challenge conventional methods of analysis and understanding in their disciplines, which often excluded a consideration of ingrained social and power perspectives that disadvantaged women.

In her book, *Academic Pathfinders* (2002), Patricia Gumport draws a useful distinction between three groups of academics: forerunners, pathfinders and pathtakers. Forerunners were those female scholars who had become established faculty prior to the so-called second wave, and were ambiguous in their reaction to the new wave of feminist scholarship. The pathfinders were more highly politicized and sought to blend activism with scholarship. They critiqued and sought to transform their fields by deploying a feminist perspective, while others put their energies into creating the new academic field of women's studies despite considerable counter-criticism from more conventional scholars. Finally, Gumport describes pathtakers. While pathfinders had fought for academic recognition and respect for feminist scholarship, pathtakers represented a new generation who could choose to either deploy or disregard this perspective as academics. In a sense, a feminist form of analysis was now normalized and not as closely associated with political activism. There is a wider point here that links being a critic with being an advocate for something (see the section below). According to Gumport (2002, p. xiii):

faculty who aspire to create knowledge must each in her or his own way become a pathfinder, engaged in an ongoing process of discovering a way through or into unexplored regions.

Being a critic needs to be understood as taking place in different contexts, from the inner world of the discipline through to the applied and societal context in which disciplines, politics and society intersect. In the French tradition, the intellectual acting as a critic in this public space is accepted as a legitimate role. Not all cultures are as approving, and attitudes in the UK lie in sharp contrast. While academics are encouraged to engage in the public space, their role tends to be seen mainly as trading their expertise for the benefit of business, the government or the community.

Universities have reinforced this more limited form of engagement by promoting policies on knowledge transfer. This represents the idea that academics should serve business, the government and society at large in a relatively passive way rather than criticizing its practices, assumptions and prevailing values. In 2009, Professor David Nutt, the chair of the UK Advisory Council on the Misuse of Drugs, criticized the government's decision to reclassify cannabis from a class C to a class B drug (Gossop and Hall, 2009). He argued that the issue of drug classification had become politicized and that the decision was not based on the evidence. Taking exception to these comments, the government minister, Alan Johnson, said he had lost confidence in Professor Nutt and sacked him from his position. It is clear that the assumptions of the minister were that the role of this academic was to serve and to be loyal to the government. He should not, in other words, bite the hand that feeds.

It is important to note that the features of intellectualism identified in this chapter do not necessitate the dominant practice of many modern academics, particularly in the human and social sciences: namely the collecting of data in the tradition of natural science. While empirical research is an important element of academic enquiry in many, especially scientific fields, it is not a *pre-condition* for adopting the identity of an intellectual. The nature of academic enquiry can be focused on a search for wisdom as much as a search for knowledge (Maxwell, 2009). Nicholas Maxwell (2009) argues that universities have become too pre-occupied with the acquisition and application of knowledge directed largely at technological growth. Knowledge inquiry, he argues, is focused on finding the truth but at the expense of 'feelings and desires, values, ideals, political and religious views, expressions of hopes and fear, cries of pain ... ' (Maxwell, 2009, p. 4). He sees the exclusion of the social and political considerations associated with the application of knowledge from the process of knowledge inquiry as illogical, and contributes little to human welfare. Instead, Maxwell contends that there needs to be more concern for what he terms wisdom inquiry focused on the problems.

Hence, being a pathfinder is about more than simply being an empirical researcher. Not all researchers challenge their own assumptions about the world or conventional wisdom in their discipline. To do this takes courage, not just intellect (Macfarlane, 2009). This demands an independence of thinking and a preparedness to take a risk. It also demands a preparedness to breach the conventions of and the boundaries between academic disciplines. Some fields have paradigms that are particularly well established or developed. Those disciplines with the highest levels of paradigm development tend to have a level of consensus that makes it least likely that dissenting voices will be listened to or tolerated. The areas of interest, research methods and tools for explanatory analysis are clear and well defined. Economics is such a field that has made it less open to feminist perspectives, for example (Gumport, 2002).

Being a critic is a privilege of academic life but, like all privileges, it is one that can be abused if it is undertaken in a merely destructive manner that fails to provide a creative alternative to the idea or practice that is being criticized. Academics are often characterized, or perhaps caricatured, as radicals. In recent years, the extent to which some members of the academic community have sought to criticize the core values of Western culture have led to a backlash from those who contend that this is destroying the basis for a liberal university education (e.g. Bloom, 1987; Kimball, 1990). The charge is that the influence of postmodernism, deconstruction and post-structural theory, in the humanities and social sciences in particular, has created a form of political correctness in the academy around the view that all knowledge is socially and politically constructed. A number of theorists, notably the French historian and philosopher Michel Foucault, are associated with the idea that knowledge is about the promotion of vested interests. This has led to a new orthodoxy emerging in universities based on the primary importance of analysing and (re)valuing the role of gender, race, class and ethnicity in understanding claims to knowledge. Critics of postmodernism such as Bloom (1987) and Kimball (1990) see such an analysis as a rejection of the canons of Western enlightenment. Kimball refers to this as a 'war against Western culture' (Kimball, 1990, p. 15). While it is easy to dismiss the claims of Bloom and Kimball from a modern sociological perspective as reactionary and defensive, part of the point they are making is that academics are acting as destructive cynics and critics rather than as creators and developers of young minds.

Professor as advocate

If one accepts that there is no such thing as objective knowledge, and the world is socially constructed, then this poses an additional, or perhaps insurmountable, barrier to anyone making any new knowledge claim. The potential creator of new knowledge must answer a series of further questions: is the argument or claim culturally bounded? Is it connected with defending vested social and political interests? Is it merely a Western perspective? Is the claim offering more than a gendered perspective? These and other questions provide a challenging framework for trying to make claims that are generalizable. Faced with questions like these, it is hardly surprising that many academics have retreated into the safer waters of empirical research, where the design of projects can build in such considerations as far as possible. Research in the modern university is now largely about empirical research rather than broader conceptual enquiry as a result. In a postmodernist age it is, in a sense, no longer politically correct to make new knowledge claims.

Yet the challenge of making new knowledge claims, however daunting, is an essential part of what it means to exercise academic freedom, and a component part of intellectual leadership. Being a critic is, in my view, not enough. One has also got to advocate something that goes beyond simply critiquing what has come before. This is about being an advocate of ideas, theories, models or arguments of some sort. While being a critic is central to what it means to be an intellectual, on its own it is not sufficient. It is also important to have 'something to say' that is constructive, not just destructive. Taking apart other peoples' ideas or concepts is one thing. Being an advocate involves offering a vision or an alternative path from the status quo. In many respects it is easier to be a critic than an advocate, since there is no need to risk one's own reputation through proposing a new theory, model, interpretation or plan. Being an intellectual implies having certain commitments that can be both theoretical and socio-political in nature. Developing a set of one's own demands intellectual and often moral courage. All too often, academics are content to be critics but either do not have the imagination or perhaps the courage to offer an alternative. To be an intellectual leader, it is essential to have a positive agenda, not just a hit list of dislikes and gripes.

While it is important to have something to claim, argue or simply say, there is always the danger of falling into the trap of making broad brush generalizations in the manner of grand theory – defined by Wright Mills (1959, p. 34) as 'the associating and disassociating of concepts'. The criticism of grand theory is that conceptual claims can overreach their empirical basis, leading to the suspicion that 'the emperor has no clothes' (Wright Mills, 1959, p. 35). Intellectuals without a research base for their arguments are often open to criticisms of grand-standing. On the other hand, becoming absorbed by the methodological detail of academic enquiry can obfuscate important messages for wider society that should emerge from the data. This other extreme is what Wright Mills labels abstracted empiricism, which shrinks from any substantive propositions or theories to focus on statistical or methodological detail. Striking a balance between these two extremes is as pertinent for the intellectual as for the academic. While empirical research is the basis for generating new knowledge, unless this knowledge is connected to a wider framework of multi-disciplinary or societal analysis, it is likely to stay within the narrow prism of disciplinary scholarship.

Advocacy is about making a connection between the knowledge base of a discipline or profession and the context of its application in practice. The study of law, for example, has a multitude of different applied sub-specialisms, such as employment, family, criminal and international law, and considerable scope for research into case histories, national systems, international treaties and so forth. There is though a clear link between the study of law and advocacy concerns. These might include access to justice for the poor, the professional conduct of lawyers, and the treatment of vulnerable groups such as refugees, prostitutes or the homeless (Rhode, 2001).

The sociologist Peter Townsend (1928–2009) was more than an academic. He became a well-known campaigner against poverty. Townsend's own background was steeped in poverty, brought up by a single mother during the 1930s and surrounded by the effects of the inter-war depression. He gained a scholarship to University College school and later developed a successful academic career, becoming a professor of sociology in 1963 at the newly founded University of Essex. His career was devoted to rigorous research into poverty and campaigning to influence government policy. In 1965 he founded the Child Poverty Action Group (CPAG) and also later co-founded the Disability Alliance. His work was influential in establishing that while absolute levels of poverty may have fallen in the post-war years, health inequalities or relative poverty had worsened. In the *Black Report* (Department of Health and Social Security, 1980), Townsend's work brought such inequalities to light, such as the widening gap between death rates according to social class. While Townsend's tireless advocacy met with only limited political success, especially during the 1980s when a Conservative government was in power, his work did have an influence internationally, leading to similar studies about health inequalities in other countries.

As Townsend's career to some extent illustrates, academic knowledge is not a static, timeless entity but a site of constantly shifting struggle for preeminence within and between disciplines. Shifting patterns of influence are affected by changes within society where so-called mode 2 knowledge is created in the context of application (Gibbons *et al.*, 1994) as much as by intellectual disputes between disciplinary groups. Within this context, advocacy can be both offensive and defensive. It can take the form of developing a new (sub)academic discipline such as women's studies (Gumport, 2002). In the process such pathfinders 'came to generate a new knowledge speciality within and outside their disciplines' (Gumport, 2002, p. xiii). A precursor to this advocacy was criticism of the absence of feminist perspectives and analysis within a range of social science disciplines before the 1960s. This is an example of how criticism and advocacy are intertwined.

Criticism and advocacy should be two sides of the same coin, in the same way that I earlier characterized academic freedom and academic duty. To criticize is to imply that there must be an alternative or perhaps better way. While Richard Dawkins is an outspoken critic of creationism, he is also an advocate for a gene-centred view of evolution and humanism. While Peter Townsend criticized definitions of poverty based on absolute criteria, he was also responsible for advocating its replacement with a relative criteria for measurement. He defined poverty as 'the absence or inadequacy of those diets, amenities, standards, services and activities which are common or customary in society' (Townsend, 1979, p. 915). The concept of relative poverty is now widely accepted, but back in the 1960s such a concept was new to many of those involved in public policy. In the 1970s, those on the political new right continued to regard and define poverty as an absolute condition, a position represented by the Conservative government of 1979 under Margaret Thatcher (Hickson, 2009). Yet by 2006, the Conservative opposition under David Cameron acknowledged that poverty should be understood as relative rather than absolute (Cameron, 2006). Townsend's advocacy of relative poverty as a concept, and the evidence he produced of relative poverty levels in reports and books, played an important role in changing minds over time.

Being an advocate implies having certain commitments that can be both conceptual or theoretical and socio-political in nature. Being an advocate for one's discipline or profession implies explaining and promoting key ideas, debating issues and lobbying on behalf of concepts. Advocacy can be quite specialized in nature, such as championing a particular theoretical perspective, or adopting a more populist position in connecting one's scholarly interests with a public campaign (e.g. women's rights, climate change or reforming penal policy). Being an advocate goes well beyond the fact that someone has researched or published a lot. It is about being, in the words of one of my respondents, an 'independent champion' of a cause. At one end of the spectrum the professor as advocate might seek to promote understanding and acceptance of an alternative theoretical paradigm in their discipline. At the other end of this spectrum, the professor as advocate might be more of a public activist campaigning for changes in public policy engaging with the popular media.

Advocacy is also about explaining, and to some extent defending, the importance of the discipline to a wider audience. A number of professors in the humanities and social sciences were conscious that their disciplines were coming under increasing pressure to justify their relevance to society in a more business-oriented era of higher education. Here, there was a recognition that explaining and advocating the importance of one's discipline was an important part of being a professor in the modern era:

> What we have to do [as professors] is to develop and defend the profession ... we need to defend the intellectual content of what we do.
>
> (professor of English)

This demands looking at ways to apply disciplinary or professional knowledge and skills for the benefit of wider public understanding through public outreach, with a range of government, non-government and charitable bodies. For the professor of English, this work meant explaining how her research, which had analysed early textual representations of one of the health professions, was relevant to how the profession defined its role today. This professor was also keen to defend her subject from criticisms based on perceptions of (a lack of) vocational relevance, arguing that 'there is no such thing as useless knowledge'.

While professors in humanities and social science fields can be concerned about public perceptions of the relevance of their discipline, professors in science are often committed to trying to improve public understanding of complex ideas. This demands engagement with members of the public in a variety of ways:

> It is important to be able to communicate at different levels. Science is a very complicated area and I think the ability to put that over to the general public is an important part of what I do ... over the weekend I spent Friday, Saturday and Sunday at a patient conference where I gave two lectures and I was on an expert panel answering questions from patients and their relatives.
>
> (professor of oncology)

Advocacy can take the form of defending the old as well as promoting the new. A number of professors, especially in the humanities and social sciences, are conscious that their disciplines are coming under increasing pressure to justify their relevance to society in a more business-oriented era of higher education. Here, there is a recognition that explaining and advocating the importance of one's discipline is an important part of being a professor in the modern era. While professors in humanities and social science fields can be concerned about public perceptions of the relevance of their discipline, professors in science are often committed to trying to improve public understanding of complex ideas. This demands engagement with members of the public in a variety of ways.

Here, what can be seen as a lack of public understanding of, or perhaps sympathy with, the importance of the discipline needed to be addressed by professors as intellectual leaders. This demands a commitment to engagement work such as writing for the popular press, being interviewed on radio or television, or making links with schools or business and community organizations.

I am not alone in identifying the importance of intellectual processes similar to the ones I have referred to under using the broad-brush terms of critic and advocate. Research on the academic identities of transnational or so-called mobile academics has identified a group labelled as 'academic intellectuals' (Kim, 2010). These individuals are said to be involved in the creative destruction and reconstruction of the paradigms of academic work (Kim, 2010). This is a parallel description of the intellectual process involved in being a critic and an advocate, the former of which involves destruction (or perhaps deconstruction) and the latter reconstruction of academic tenets.

Boundary transgression

Intellectual leadership is not just about being a keen critic and advocate within the confines of the discipline. It is also about moving beyond the comfort zone of subject specialism. This involves traversing the boundaries of disciplines and often seeking to redefine academic knowledge in the process. Sometimes this is referred to as trans-disciplinarity. I label this role as being a boundary transgressor (see Chapter 9).

University environments are premised on the organization of academics within disciplinary groupings. As such they tend to reinforce intellectual boundaries between disciplines. Those that stray outside discipline boundaries are often punished in a variety of ways. Notably their scholarship can be unfashionable and result in reduced chances to gain funding and publication, inhibiting career progression in the process. Those that transgress the norms of methodological investigation in the discipline can face further barriers. A boundary transgressor can be rejected by their own or original discipline and face difficulties in being accepted by other disciplines too. Disciplines can act as closed communities, and the boundaries are often strictly patrolled to keep out those from elsewhere.

However, being a critic and an advocate are closely related and come together through a process sometimes referred to as boundary transgression. This can take many different forms. An intellectual might seek to cross the boundaries between disciplines, forging a new specialism in the process. Sociologists who enter the world of science are variously described as 'boundary transgressors', 'hybrids' and 'classification confusers' (Bauchspies *et al.*, 2006, p. 98). Another challenging and difficult task is to cross methodological boundaries, especially when, by tradition, 'most disciplines are quick to police their boundaries against methodological transgressions' (Gordon, 2009, p. 18). Intellectuals often operate from multiple rather than single disciplinary perspectives, and are also boundary transgressors in terms of wishing to operate both within an academic context and across more public forums for debate and dissemination. Intellectuals tend to see knowledge as a public good rather than a private commodity. Ken Green (1946–2009), a professor of environmental innovation management at the University of Manchester, was someone who was a boundary transgressor through his advocacy of studying the role of science in society in science courses:

> He personified a style of academic inquiry informed by interdisciplinary knowledge and social commitment – a vital combination that is becoming less and less visible in the modern university landscape.
>
> (Reisz, 2009a, p. 27)

Like inventors, intellectuals have to be boundary transgressors, because they are prepared to 'unthink' what they already know and retain a desire for new experiences. They are ready to abandon their previous beliefs in order to continue to be creative individuals. This is about recognizing that the acquisition of knowledge is as much an emotional as a cognitive process. Learning can represent 'loss' in the sense that it can imply the replacement of previous beliefs with new ones, rather than simply the acquisition of 'more' knowledge. Learning something new can, in other words, be supplantive and not additive. In a later chapter (see Chapter 9) I will return to the concept of boundary transgressors as one of four orientations to intellectual leadership.

Conclusion

Being a critic and an advocate are preconditions for intellectual leadership. They are not the sole prerogative of the professoriate and on their own they do not make someone an intellectual leader, but they are essential if others are going to look to someone for leadership. These freedoms need to be balanced in two ways. First, this privilege needs to be exercised within the rules of rational discourse. It is not a licence to make personal or insulting remarks about others, only to critique ideas, theories and discourses and other claims to originality or intellectual insight. Criticism must be justified and, where possible and appropriate, evidence-based. Second, academic freedom is only one dimension of the professor as intellectual leader. This needs to be balanced and complemented by the flipside of the coin: academic duty. The chapter that follows will outline these complementary duties and why they are important to intellectual leadership.

Chapter 8

Four duties

Introduction

The previous chapter focused on the freedoms of intellectual leadership and the importance of establishing a credible reputation through criticism and advocacy. There are iconoclastic individuals in academic life who have achieved these things and are widely respected on this basis. They are intellectuals but they are not all considered necessarily to be intellectual *leaders*. It is not, in other words, enough to be a thinker and an activist. Sometimes such individuals can offer what Trow (2010a) and others have labelled symbolic leadership. Their ideas or personality become the focus of attention; a rallying point for a group of individuals or a movement. Possessing the qualities of leadership though is about more than intelligent analysis and the courage and confidence to speak out. A leader must have a commitment through action to work with others in a way that inspires and serves. They need a generosity of spirit and a desire to serve others. In an academic context, this may be expressed as a commitment and a facility for *academic duty*.

This chapter will examine characteristics or traits that form the key components of academic duty. On the basis of the feedback I received from my interviewees and questionnaire respondents, these traits may be summarized as being *a mentor, a guardian, an enabler* and *an ambassador*. A professor needs to be committed to these roles, in addition to possessing a strong reputation based on their academic work, if they are going to be regarded as an intellectual leader. The emphasis on individual performance and achievements in the development of academics means that these qualities cannot be automatically assumed. Being an able mentor, or a person sufficiently motivated to uphold standards of scholarship within the discipline through peer review, demands a commitment to others. These traits require both experience and a moral commitment to the development of the discipline. The only real formal training that most professors (or indeed most academics) receive for their role is the doctorate. Informally as much, if not more, is learnt by working with academic colleagues, including doctoral supervisors, who can be influential role models. Here, the emphasis, especially in the humanities and social sciences, is on lone scholarship rather than the development of a broader set of skills and dispositions that support academic duty. This is why the traits of academic duty cannot be taken for granted.

Academic duty

While academic freedom attracts widespread attention both in academic thought and in the popular press, academic duty is a less visible but nonetheless fundamental feature of academic life. It is every bit as essential as academic freedom. This is because the production of knowledge and the teaching of students is a cooperative process. It necessitates a collegial infrastructure on which everything else depends. This is partly about belonging to an 'invisible college' (Halsey and Trow, 1971; Barnett, 1990) through which academics share intellectual connections via informal relationships that link institutions and disciplines. Academics have obligations to their students, to their immediate colleagues, to their disciplinary peers, to their institutions, and to the wider public with whom they want to communicate their ideas (Macfarlane, 2007). This set of obligations involves processes that demand an unselfish attitude of contributing to the understanding of others through activities, such as giving feedback to a student, mentoring a colleague, reviewing a paper for publication, serving on a university committee, working as an external examiner or advising a government minister. These examples illustrate the gamut of academic duty and activities that attract varying degrees of prestige. They are all, though, about sacrificing time that might otherwise be spent on more self-regarding and better rewarded activities, such as personal research and publication or paid consultancy. Even the lone scholar depends on her or his peers to review their papers for publications, to write reviews about their books, or to introduce their students to their work. Academic life, in short, depends on cooperation. Without this, the whole enterprise would falter.

Conventionally, the word service has often been used to invoke the kind of activities that I refer to under the heading of academic duty. The phrase academic citizenship has also been coined (Shils, 1997; Macfarlane, 2007). In recent years, though, the modern university appears to have turned its back on the importance of service as the third element of its mission alongside teaching and research. A more business and commercially oriented lexicon has entered the university. Knowledge transfer or knowledge exchange has become part of the mission of universities in the UK, Hong Kong and elsewhere in the world. In part, this trend is prompted by governments, and their respective funding councils, seeking evidence for the way in which the university adds value to the economy. Universities are under pressure to demonstrate that they deserve continued public funding. The problem though with this new language is that it erodes the sense in which academics are responsible towards others on an individual, *pro bono* basis. In short, it encourages a shift toward a business-oriented culture where all activities are evaluated for their commercial, rather than social and moral, value (see Chapter 10).

Yet, in practice, to be an intellectual leader demands a commitment to academic duty: a desire to help others without the expectation necessarily of an exchange value or *quid pro quo*. It necessitates a selfless disposition and skills that will enable others to develop. It is about full participation in, and making a contribution to, building intellectual communities often associated with the discipline.

Role model

How can these academic duties be described? The starting point before describing duties is that, in an overarching sense, a professor needs to be a good role model. They must be a good example to other academics able to demonstrate what it means to be not just an ordinary academic, but a very good one. In part, this means having a well-respected scholarly reputation with achievements to match. It also implies a range of other qualities, such as being a respected teacher, possibly holding a formal role as a leader, or contributing informally in a variety of ways. The ways in which professors contribute informally in leading others has a good deal to do with the tacit expectations connected with academic duty.

A considerable challenge for the modern day professor lies in the extent to which they seek to be a role model across a wide range of activities. Despite attempts to raise the status of teaching in many contexts, and the growing responsibilities of management in modern higher education, as we have seen their personal excellence in research still remains the principal reason for their appointment as a professor. As I illustrated in Chapter 6 there are now, in reality, many different types of professor. Despite this, most professors that I spoke with or heard from said they need to be role models across most, if not all, aspects of the academic role. They want to be excellent researchers, inspirational teachers as well as capable managers. Here, there was a vision of the professor as a meta-academic, an exemplar who possesses the credibility upon which to lead. Here are a few of the descriptions of the way that professors see the role:

> A productive and high-impact scholar and inspirational teacher with good administrative and managerial skills who has a real interest in fostering the personal and collective development of colleagues (both within their immediate remit and outside of it). Somebody with foresight, energy, and optimism, who is both internally and externally engaged, and is up-to-date with current developments in academia nationally and globally.
>
> (professor of law)

> [A professor] should be a model of professional expertise and knowledge, an example of dealing with the complexities of academic work (research, teaching and managerial duties).
>
> (professor of history)

> A professor should be a leader in his subject area of research. Inevitably, professors are asked to become managers of their section, department, etc.

I also believe professors should strive to be good teachers and should be able to foster scholarship and excellence in teaching in their subject area.

(professor of English)

Academic and administrative expertise; fund raising and mentoring young staff; facilitating research of older staff; establishing national and international collaborations and obtaining funding for this; providing earned income for the university.

(professor of oncology)

These are idealistic portraits of the professor as a role model across all elements of academic practice. A professor must, in other words, be capable of doing it all. But is this realistic? Some professors do not think so, and believe that a distinction needs to be made between academic leadership and management. Here, the professor is defined as a field or subject specialist or expert rather than possessing more all-round abilities.

There was recognition among some respondents and interviewees that professors can be poor role models as well as good ones in practice. Professors falling short in this area of academic duty were seen as those with a lack of commitment to helping others or prepared to carry out their fair share of teaching and administrative duties. Professors, in other words, should do things as a good citizen and not just focus on their individual research interests:

Some people are extremely selfish and only do things to benefit their own research activity.

(professor of engineering)

... it is difficult to get professors to take responsibility to do things unless they are really interested and they have benefit (i.e. for them) or by nature they have an attitude as a team player.

(professor of management)

The Dean [said] this guy [a professor] is fantastic, 'you just have to lock him in a cage and rattle that cage once a week and get a paper out' but you couldn't let him talk to the students or anything and I don't think that my subject area in the UK is big enough to absorb those sorts of people.

(professor of accountancy)

The notion of acting as a role model, and having credibility, mirrors one of the 13 forms of 'leader behaviours' identified by Bryman in his meta-analysis of the literature about leadership in higher education (Bryman, 2007). In other words, having academic standing is a prerequisite. However, being a role model is still largely associated with the qualifications needed to become a professor. In *being* a professor, respondents referred to additional qualities.

Professor as mentor

Overwhelmingly, professors spoke to me about the importance attached to being a mentor to less experienced colleagues, through encouraging and nurturing the potential of others. The language used to describe being a mentor varied, including words such as 'facilitator', 'guide to others' and 'nurturer'. An interviewee explained that the practical reality of her role as a mentor was that it had cost her 'a fortune in taking people for coffee'. More poetically, another respondent described his motto as a leader in terms of a Welsh proverb, 'a fo ben bid bont', meaning that 'the person who would be a leader must also be a bridge', i.e. a bridge to assist people to develop – even if this means leaving the organization. This encapsulates the idea that good mentorship involves helping people realize their own potential and putting their personal interests above those of the organization they are currently working for. The word mentoring was used frequently by nearly all the professors I spoke to, or who responded to the survey. A number of examples were given of practices that were considered as constituting this type of activity:

- advising on sources of funding;
- advising on publication outlets for research;
- co-supervision of PhD students with a less experienced colleague;
- co-authorship;
- applying for research grants with less experienced colleagues;
- sitting on an external fellowship panel;
- helping colleagues to try again if they have had a paper or grant proposal rejected;
- advising on long-term career development.

The importance of the mentoring role related to the stage at which respondents had become professors. Greater importance was attached to this role by those professors who had become professors in their mid-to-late career. Some of these professors felt that their best academic work was probably behind them, and they were nearing the end of their career, so they placed more emphasis on the notion of mentoring as a means of passing on the benefit of their experience to others. This was especially notable among some female professors, who felt that the delay in their achieving professorial status, due to various forms of direct and indirect discrimination, meant that they had already enjoyed their best and most productive years. These individuals were also motivated by the desire to try to nurture women, in particular, in order to give more opportunity for the next generation of female academics to break through the professorial glass ceiling.

A number of respondents identified the importance of the professor acting as someone who nurtures colleagues with potential. Part of this role was regarded as being a talent-spotter, able to point colleagues in the right direction. Often this involves getting colleagues to take intellectual risks described by one interviewee as 'giving them the confidence to fly and jump off, when they think there might not be a safety net'. Other comments that represent this perspective include the following:

> ... securing and harnessing the intellectual capital of those members of the university within your purview.
>
> (professor of computer science)

> My view is that professors should have an organic role to play as an intellectual leader and motivator ...
>
> (professor of mathematics)

Academic obituaries often refer to the commitment of leading professors to mentorship as part of their teaching and service activities (see Chapter 9). The legacy of the evolutionary biologist Michael Majerus (1954–2009), for example, was described as 'not only in terms of the scientific contributions that he made, but also in teaching and mentoring the evolutionary biologists of tomorrow' (Reisz, 2009b). The supervision of doctoral students plays a significant part in the mentoring activities of many professors. Fred Halliday (1946–2010) supervised 62 to successful completion during his career as a professor specializing in international relations (Reisz, 2010b).

Another perception connected with mentoring was that the professor should act as a kind of 'buffer', protecting colleagues from some of the internal and external pressures faced by academics in terms of institutional demands:

> I tried to create a situation in which colleagues and students could best flourish. This entailed, negatively, being a buffer between them and internal and external pressures ...
>
> (professor of marketing)

The role of mentor is a defining quality of a good academic. It is, at root, about a commitment to inter-generational equity, but to some extent it is also about leaving a legacy, both personal and scholarly. There are, though, potential risks associated with the mentoring role. One of these is that the mentee becomes overly dependent on the mentor. This might occur in an intellectual sense inasmuch as they are not just influenced but become a devotee or uncritical disciple of the mentor. Here, it is important that the professor as mentor encourages their mentee to become independent minded in their intellectual interests and affiliations. In practice this is a difficult balancing act to achieve, since mentoring tends to engender, especially where the mentor is a doctoral supervisor, a strong sense of loyalty. However, as with all good teaching relationships, success comes when the student, or in this case the mentee, is no longer intellectually dependent on the mentor and finds their own voice. The professor as mentor has succeeded when the mentee no longer needs their support and guidance.

Professor as guardian

A second quality associated with professorial leadership is being a guardian (or steward) of academic standards and associated values. These include the established tenets and conventions of the discipline or profession. Upholding the principles of good scholarship is a key part of the responsibilities of senior academics when working as editors, peer reviewing contributions to journals or in undertaking any number of other gatekeeping or *pro bono* activities, such as examining doctoral candidates or reviewing papers, that determine who receives recognition and advancement in their discipline or professional field.

Being a guardian is part of a professor's good citizen role. In many respects it represents the shift in role that takes place when someone becomes a professor. Whilst becoming a professor demands a focus on a great deal of (often individualized) personal achievement, being a professor implies undertaking reciprocal duties such as reviewing and editing. To some extent this is a natural process. Research-active academics, regardless of whether they are professors, normally acquire an increasing number of guardianship duties or responsibilities as they become more experienced and better known in their field. However, as respondents and interviewees made clear, not all professors are prepared to 'give back' in this way.

An implicit part of guardianship is ensuring that the next generation of academics are inculcated with an appropriate set of values and academic standards inherent to the discipline. There is a desire, as one professor expressed it, to 'pass on the baton'. Here, professors are concerned about what might be termed succession planning; ensuring their own research interests are taken forward by younger colleagues following their own retirement. There is some overlap here with mentoring, but guardianship also involves ensuring that the next generation not only succeed but continue to preserve the structures and standards that have been established:

> I think it is necessary to, when we are looking at a research structure, to have people coming through the ranks and aspiring to the next step on the ladder. Otherwise when you drop off the edge, if you don't have anyone else in that discipline, that discipline just dies ...
>
> (professor of oncology)

> ... the whole of the professoriate should be very conscious of bringing on the next generation of the academy because although they would like to professors do not go on forever.
>
> (professor of law)

This element of guardianship is about ensuring continuity and the survival of disciplinary specialisms in an increasingly competitive world of epistemological fragmentation. As a young researcher, a professor will have benefited from having had their own papers and research grant proposals reviewed by more senior colleagues. By the time someone becomes a professor (or perhaps in some instances well before) it is now their turn to take on or contribute more in relation to this academic duty. This does not mean though that such activities are entirely selfless. While membership of editorial boards or research councils is rarely remunerated, except occasionally in nominal terms, they have a prestige value that is valuable to an ambitious academic.

As with mentorship there are risks attached. The professor as guardian is often in a powerful position as a reviewer of grant proposals or journal papers. Here, great care needs to be taken to avoid the temptation, for example, to reject manuscripts that do not conform to a particular theoretical or methodological stance that the reviewer might favour. The professor as guardian needs to distinguish carefully between academic work with which they might disagree, and that which, more straightforwardly, represents poor scholarship. Some reviewers gain warranted reputations as 'assassins' (Siegelman, 1991) who apply unreasonably exacting standards, while others, referred to as 'zealots', represent the other extreme of behaviour by accepting manuscripts without examining them with sufficient rigour. Hence, the role of professor as guardian involves moral dilemmas and a need to find a median position between these extremes. Being a gatekeeper for a discipline demands both the maintenance of high standards whilst retaining open-mindedness and a desire to encourage the development of the field in new directions.

Professor as enabler

Being a facilitator or an enabler is an extension of mentoring in the sense that it involves opening up opportunities for others to do research, meet influential academic colleagues and generally provide chances for collaboration. It is about collaborative networking. An important part of this function is giving others access or an entrée to networks of other scholars. This involves professors in using their social capital (Bourdieu, 1986), in the sense of resources based on membership groups, relationships and influential and durable networks. A professor's recommendation or introduction can be part of a process of gaining acceptance into the wider academic community. This type of activity is often seen at academic conferences through co-presentation of papers, where one of the authors is a junior colleague (often a doctoral student or post-doctoral fellow), and the other might be a more established figure in the field. Professors are aware that networking is critical to their own influence and to that of other academics who wish to advance in their careers. They even invoked the language of Bourdieu in explanation:

> Too often colleagues think it [i.e. being a successful academic] is about publishing more when actually it is undertaking service that enables one to network and form social and political capital.

> (professor of economics)

An important role is fostering collaborations between colleagues you know ... putting people in touch and so on.

(professor of education)

I always saw my role as a facilitator ... never ceasing to look for ways of advancing and encouraging individuals and groups.

(professor of fine art)

Informally, networking can result in opportunities being presented to less experienced academics by more senior academics, such as involvement in peer review, brokering invitations to speak at seminars or conferences or simply informal conversations, both online and face to face. Electronically processed information networks are now critical to understanding the way that social structures and activities form and work in practice (Castells, 2000). However, whilst network technologies make it easier than ever for academics at all levels to link up with others within and beyond their field, professors still play an important role in being gatekeepers of, and providing access to, the most prestigious networks and contacts.

Being an enabler is about more than effecting introductions. It also involves generating resources and income. This provides a means that allows others to participate, especially in research activities, and leads to the employment of research assistants and other junior or inexperienced academics as part of project teams. Most professors did not regard income generation as a high priority compared with the emphasis that their institutions placed on such achievements. However, they were aware that attracting grants, contracts and other resources were an integral part of a new commercial reality regardless of discipline. Without income generation a professor will have a diminished impact as an enabler. Creating research centres and winning research grants means that professors can give opportunities to more doctoral students and employ more pre- and post-doctoral research assistants. This increases their intellectual influence over others. Professors with research centres and substantial research grants are likely to have bigger networks of influence. Resources bring the power to influence and also, to some extent, the power of independence from other institutional demands such as management and teaching.

Being an enabler is closely related to supporting younger researchers and research teams. A number of professors explained that while their role was, in part, to acquire research grants, these funds were necessary to support their less experienced colleagues and research assistants, whose time could be calculated on a more affordable economic basis. Hence, professors can find themselves in a position where their own time is too expensive to conduct research and act principally as an attractor of funds and in writing up papers for publication:

I do very little real research myself now ... my role mainly involves getting research grants and project management.

(professor of biochemistry)

There may be less expectation of acquisition of grants and other resources for professors in some areas of the arts or humanities, for example, than in the bio-medical sciences. Similarly, some professorial appointments are closely linked to areas of public and social policy where an individual might be expected to play a more visible role as an advocate, for example. Professors in science areas, where team-based working is the norm, tend to face this pressure more strongly. As I reported in Chapter 5 based on my survey data, they are more likely than their counterparts in the arts and humanities to see income generation as a legitimate part of their role. In part this is also attributable to the need for major funding in order to conduct scientific research, while the concern of professors in the arts and humanities is mainly about securing time to do research. They tend to see income generation as a means of justifying their use of time rather than in supporting a wider team or in building up equipment or laboratory facilities.

There are, of course, risks that being an enabler can slip into the realms of nepotism or what is sometimes termed cronyism. Here rather than simply effecting introductions and seeking to help others to network, such activities can become directed at seeking preferential treatment for favoured former students or junior colleagues, rather than on the basis of their academic merit alone. In Chinese culture the benefits derived from social connections are described as *guanxi* and this plays an important role in academic life. Whilst academic duty would suggest that being an enabler is a selfless activity in practice it can involve the expectation of reciprocation.

Professor as ambassador

Finally, in an external facing capacity, some respondents referred to the importance of the professor acting as an *ambassador* on behalf of the university, representing its interests on the national and international stage.

Being visible or 'out and about' were seen as vital activities for a professor, to both maintain their national and international profile and as a means of promoting the reputation of the university. Examples given of this type of activity included keynote addresses at academic conferences and participating in international recruitment and research collaboration with other universities or commercial organizations. These activities were regarded as a means of providing the university with a higher public and sector-wide profile. Here, there is perhaps some crossover with the advocate role (see Chapter 7). Being an ambassador, though, implies promoting the university and the department, whereas being an advocate was associated more closely with promoting conceptual and socio-political perspectives often connected closely with the discipline:

> [Being a professor] ... denotes that by definition one is deemed a leading figure in one's discipline as well as someone capable of representing one's institution, both internally and externally.
>
> (professor of law)

We [as professors] can contribute to raising the profile of our institutions by our academic and research activities.

(professor of oncology)

However, many professors do not necessarily rate this quality as highly. Ask an academic what their main point of identity is and they will reply that it is their discipline, first and foremost. Loyalty to their institution comes often a very poor second. This is borne out by an international study of the academic profession carried out in 2007 (Locke, 2007). This pattern is most apparent (and extreme) among academics from countries with so-called 'mature' higher education systems such as Australia, Canada, Japan, Norway, the UK and the United States; 80 per cent of faculty in these countries considered their affiliation to their discipline to be either fairly or very important. By contrast, asked about their commitment to their institution, the figures look very different. Just 57 per cent of academics from these mature systems considered institutional affiliation fairly or very important. In many ways this finding is unsurprising as, like other professionally qualified people, academics are focused on their professional identity rather than institutional objectives.

Table 8.1 summarizes the academic duties associated with professorial leadership. Collectively, they incorporate a commitment as both a local, in serving the institution, and a cosmopolitan, in contributing toward the development of the discipline or profession. This suggests that professors see themselves as 'cosmo-locals' (Goldberg, 1976), with an orientation that combines commitment to both internal and external communities, or in the mould of 'rooted cosmopolitans' as suggested by Nixon (2010b).

It is important to recognize that this is an idealized set of academic duties. In practice, it is challenging for all professors to necessarily live out all these qualities. Quite apart from differences in personality, respondents recognized there are different types of professors (see Chapter 6). This disaggregation means that professors are seen more as specialists rather than all-rounders. Hence, a research (or star) professor might be expected to attract more resources than, say, a managerial professor, who might in turn spend more time in ambassadorial roles

Table 8.1 Four duties of professorial leadership

Mentor	To less experienced colleagues within and without the institution
Guardian	Of standards of scholarship and academic values within the discipline or profession
Enabler	Of opportunities for others through providing access to networks, funding grants, collaborations including the acquisition of grants, contracts and other commercial opportunities
Ambassador	On behalf of the university in external relations both nationally and internationally

for the institution, promoting its image, forging new partnerships with a view to course expansion and recruiting students. At root, though, one might expect all professors to demonstrate most of these academic duties, especially mentoring and guardianship of standards.

The importance of legacy

In this, and the previous chapter, I have sought to identify the core qualities of intellectual leadership – critic, advocate, mentor, guardian, enabler and ambassador. Such a list of qualities is daunting for any one person to possess. Hence, I want to add a note of realism. Here, it is important to emphasize that not all intellectual leaders necessarily possess all of these traits. Even great leaders have weaknesses. Some have strengths in particular areas, such as advocacy of a particular position or an ability to mentor others. There is also likely to be some shifting of emphasis between these traits according to the stage at which someone finds themselves. Although this may not be the case for everyone, a more senior figure, toward the end of their academic career, might be likely to focus on the qualities connected with academic duty, while a less experienced or younger professor will tend to be more concerned with making their mark via critique and advocacy, and may not necessarily have yet developed the full set of skills, or dispositions, associated with academic duty.

The problem with most lists of qualities, such as the one I have presented, is that there are always others that may be added. Intellectual leadership is a concept that is remarkably hard to capture. Any list of qualities cannot do the concept justice, since it involves an amalgam of skill, experience and a hard-to-define capacity. In the entertainment world, talent shows try to identify the performer who stands out from others by dint of an X factor: a special gift that can be recognized in practice but rarely described in theory. An X factor is something that makes a performer different. Amongst all the other participants their voice or skill is memorable. This is what makes a star. It involves a talent to stand out and to be recognized.

The X factor for intellectual leaders is about legacy. This word is commonly associated with property or money left by someone in their will. Here though I am referring to a person's intellectual work or associated achievements, as they are remembered and continue to have an impact on thinking or practice. Legacy can be both tangible and intangible. A tangible legacy might be a body of research, or perhaps, more memorably, a key concept, theory or argument for which someone is remembered. It might also be connected with student learning or the curriculum, such as an integrated curriculum or an innovative teaching technique that someone is especially associated with or is considered to have pioneered. An intangible legacy might be the influence that someone has had as a mentor on the intellectual thinking of another scholar, often evidenced through subsequent citation or acknowledgement.

Legacy means that sometimes people can be regarded as great intellectual leaders in retrospect rather than during their lifetime. Their work might gain limited recognition whilst they are alive but subsequently prove to be considerably more influential. The work of many great artists, such as Vincent Van Gogh, only gained critical and popular recognition, for example, after their death. Cardinal Newman's lectures in Dublin, that later formed the basis for *The Idea of a University*, were at first neglected but subsequently became a highly regarded articulation of a liberal ideal of university education (Brock, 1996). In more recent times, the work of Germaine Greer, particularly the sustained influence of her book *The Female Eunuch* (Greer, 1970), established her as one of the most influential feminists. Other figures can have a big impact for a shorter time, such as the anti-globalization campaigner Naomi Klein, who rose to prominence with her book *No Logo* in 2000 (Klein, 2000). Whilst Klein was listed as the eleventh most prominent public intellectual in a 2005 poll, her name did not even appear in the top 100 when the same exercise was repeated in 2008 (Prospect, 2008). Hence, it can be hard to predict who will have a significant legacy and who will not. Some figures might appear to be important during their lifetime but can prove to be less influential in death than they were in life. This might suggest that intellectual leadership is not something that can be ascribed too readily to anyone. The only real judge is time.

The nature of academic legacy is to some extent discipline related. Academics in the social sciences are often known for one key idea or concept. An example is the sociologist Stanley Cohen. He is famously associated with the notion of 'moral panics', which occur, according to his analysis, when a 'condition, episode, person or group of persons emerges to become defined as a threat to societal values and interests' (Cohen, 1972, p. 9). The mass media and establishment figures in society line up to variously analyse and condemn a phenomenon that they regard with approbation, such as football hooligans or Hell's Angels. In reality, many concepts associated with one particular academic or theorist are in themselves derived previously from other theories or ideas. Concepts, like any other form of knowledge, build on each other. Sometimes concepts supplant rather than add to existing knowledge, they replace an old idea with a new one. A good example of this is the concept of relative poverty that replaced the absolute definition of poverty. Here, the work of the sociologist Peter Townsend was significant in changing understanding and attitudes (see Chapter 7).

Rather than trying to self-ascribe primacy, many ethically grounded scholars take pains to explain that they are drawing on previous work but often, despite such assiduousness, they nonetheless become associated with the concept, idea or phrase. An example of this is the way that the sociologist Robert Merton will always be remembered for the concept of the self-fulfilling prophecy (Merton, 1948) among other ideas (e.g. the Matthew effect). Merton points out at the beginning of his essay that he owes an intellectual debt to various writers, in particular to W.I. Thomas, who stated that if men define situations as real they can have real consequences. Merton develops the idea of the self-fulfilling prophecy from this basis, arguing that falsely defined situations can lead to patterns of behaviour that can ultimately make the false definition come true. He illustrates the point by giving the example of a financially sound bank, which is subject to a false rumour that it is short of capital. This false rumour creates a panic as people rush to withdraw their money, as a result of which the bank does end up going out of business. Yet over 60 years later, it is Merton, not Thomas, who is seen as the real creator of this concept.

Conclusion

There are those that argue we live in a therapy culture, one in which assumptions of vulnerability prevail (Furedi, 2004; Ecclestone and Hayes, 2009). According to this critique, modern society is too ready to medicalize normal episodes of stress and is too focused on discourse about human emotion. Assumptions surrounding these concerns have resulted, so the thesis goes, in the phenomenon of 'helicopter' parents and a significant expansion of mental health and counselling services for university students. In a similar vein, it may be argued that the qualities or traits associated with academic duty identified in this chapter, particularly the role of mentor, are characteristic of the assumptions of a therapy culture. However, here it is important to emphasize that this set of qualities is intended as an indicator of a balanced approach to the provision of support and development. Some of the qualities demand what might be termed tough love. Mentoring involves not just the display of sympathy or empathy but honest feedback, which might, on occasions, be highly critical. Similarly, guardianship is about striking a balance between encouraging new ideas and approaches to knowledge with a concern to ensure that standards of scholarship are preserved and respected in the process. The operation of these duties are not, therefore, about being 'soft', but largely about being committed to inter-generational equity in ensuring that opportunities to support and nurture the next generation of scholars are taken seriously as part of someone's role as a professor.

The duties described above relate to the role of a professor both within and external to the university. In the internet age, the colleagues professors look to support and nurture may just as easily be on another continent as in an adjacent office. Some degree of balance though is important in ensuring that professors contribute not just to the wider development of their discipline or profession but also to the internal life of the institution they work for. Professors need to be connected both to the local and to the cosmopolitan context. If they are seen as lacking in commitment to the institutional context, professors are likely to have little influence at the local level and there is a strong chance they will be disconnected from leadership. On the other hand, it is also important for professors to avoid the other extreme: being regarded as locals but with insufficiently strong scholarly influence and networks beyond the walls of the institution. This lack of credibility will undermine the extent that they can truly be considered intellectual leaders.

In thinking through what it means to be a professor, this section of the book has identified the way they are appointed (Chapter 5), the roles they play in practice (Chapter 6), and their freedoms and duties (Chapters 7 and 8). The concluding section of the book will consider how intellectual leadership can be recovered. It will propose a model of intellectual leadership (Chapter 9), consider how universities can play a more positive role in offering intellectual leadership at the corporate level (Chapter 10) and identify ways they might make better use of their professoriate as intellectual leaders (Chapter 11).

Part 4

Reengagement

Understanding intellectual leadership

Introduction

There are both freedoms and duties connected with intellectual leadership that I have outlined in the preceding section of the book. Being a professor involves striking a necessary balance between these rights and responsibilities. Yet there are differences in the contexts in which these rights and responsibilities are likely to be exercised. Professors do not all regard their purposes in the same way, and these variations are linked to their interpretation of freedom and duty and whether they see the focus of their role as the discipline or in terms of wider civic engagement.

This chapter will identify and discuss four forms of intellectual leadership: *knowledge producer*, *academic citizen*, *boundary transgressor* and *public intellectual*. These forms or orientations might be expected of a full professor but are not exclusive to this group of academics. Other senior academics may provide intellectual leadership without necessarily being a professor. Moreover, as I have previously stated but wish to reemphasize, it needs to be acknowledged that not all professors are, in practice, intellectual leaders. This cannot be self-ascribed or simply assumed on the basis that someone holds a university chair. While a managerial professor (see Chapter 6) may be able to demonstrate the qualities associated of an intellectual leader, the organizational power they hold by dint of office is insufficient in itself. Power does not equate with intellectual authority. Similarly, a research professor without a commitment to academic duty (see Chapter 8) might be regarded as an intellectual but not necessarily an intellectual leader.

In illustrating my four forms of intellectual leadership I will draw on academic obituaries. These sketches give an insight into the key achievements of leading academics during their lifetime. They provide an example of the way that a particular scholar demonstrated an orientation toward one particular form of intellectual leadership. It is recognized, though, that many individuals might demonstrate more than a single orientation, and that during the course of an academic career patterns can shift as individuals mature and the focus of their work changes. Despite the limitation of obituaries as part eulogy, part biography, they still provide a useful insight into why academics were admired, both in respect to their scholarly and personal attributes. Obituaries can also yield some quantitative indicators of what counts in terms of the intellectual leadership offered by academics. Of 57 obituaries examined, I found that the word 'research' or 'researcher' occurred most often (92 times), followed by 'teacher' or 'teaching' (33 times) and finally 'management' (8 times). This confirms that while accomplishments in teaching and management are not unimportant, it is primarily research that defines academic achievement.

Two dimensions

The model of intellectual leadership I wish to present has two dimensions. The first of these are attitudes to the exercise of academic freedom. The second concerns whether academic duty is exercised largely by reference to the discipline or by reference to a wider societal frame.

The first dimension of my model – academic freedom – draws on an important distinction between two ways of viewing this principle. The first view is that freedom to conduct research and to teach without fear of interference, punishment or dismissal is necessary in order for academics to work effectively. Without these freedoms they cannot fulfil their role, as the basis upon which academics speak and write is their subject expertise in whatever field they happen to specialize. Hence this is a *functional view* of academic freedom (Coleman, 1977). An alternative and broader view is that in addition to being entitled to speak and write about their discipline, academics should be permitted to engage in any public issue as a citizen beyond the immediate expertise of their discipline. This might potentially extend into all areas of public discussion and debate. This is a *civic participation view* (Coleman, 1977) otherwise known as 'extramural freedom' (Metzger, 1988, p. 1265).

Hence, academic freedom can be thought of as either consisting of two elements – to teach and to research – or of three – also including engagment in extramural discussion. These elements were originally encapsulated in the American Association of University Professors' (AAUP) 1915 statement on academic freedom. The matter reportedly caused considerable debate within the committee of 15 professors that drew up this statement (Metzger, 1988). Some on the committee felt that a professor's public utterances should only be protected when they addressed issues that fell within their acknowledged area of expertise. Another criticism was that if such a privilege was claimed for university professors, this would give more protection to a professor than to a private citizen. However, despite these objections, an influential member of the committee, Arthur Lovejoy, persuaded the other members to vote for a comprehensive definition to include civic participation (Metzger, 1988). As a result, the final report included a three-fold definition that included 'extramural' academic freedom:

> Academic freedom in this sense comprises three elements: freedom of inquiry and research; freedom of teaching within the university or college; and freedom of extramural utterance and action.
>
> (AAUP, 1915, p. 292)

Part of the rationale given for the inclusion of extramural freedom in the report was that in the previous five cases of academic freedom the committee had dealt with, all had involved, at least to some extent, 'the right of university teachers to express their opinions freely outside the university or engage in political activities in their capacity as citizens' (AAUP 1915, p. 292). Although the AAUP has subsequently published further statements about academic freedom, notably in 1940, the assertion of extramural freedom has not been rescinded (Metzger, 1988).

There is much written about academic freedom but this rarely contains a discussion about extramural freedom. Often it is not specifically excluded or sanctioned, and one view is that academics enjoy the same freedom as do any other citizen to express their opinion on a matter of public interest. However, there is an important conceptual difference between offering an opinion as a private citizen and offering the same opinion in the capacity of a university professor from a respected institution. The latter can add weight or influence based on presumed authority and expertise.

In the UK, the Education Reform Act (1988) states that academics have 'freedom within the law to question and test received wisdom, and to put forward new ideas and controversial or unpopular opinions, without placing themselves in jeopardy of losing their jobs or privileges they may have at their institutions' (quoted in Karran, 2007, p. 296). What this and many other definitions of academic freedom fail to clarify is whether this includes or excludes utterances beyond the discipline of the professor. Even groups that campaign for academic freedom do not make their position entirely clear on this subject. The lobby group known as *Academics for Academic Freedom*, for example, contend that 'academics should be unrestricted both inside and outside the classroom, have unrestricted liberty to question and test received wisdom and to put forward controversial and unpopular opinions, whether or not these are deemed offensive'. The campaign website adds that 'academic institutions have no right to curb the exercise of this freedom by members of their staff, or to use it as grounds for disciplinary action or dismissal' (Academics for Academic Freedom, 2011). However, this statement does not make it crystal clear whether or not 'unrestricted liberty' is defined in terms of expression of opinions connected with the discipline, or includes statements of opinions unconnected with subject expertise.

The distinction between academic freedom to teach and research a discipline is a more limited definition of this concept than one that also includes extramural freedom. Hence the first dimension in my model of intellectual leadership concerns what I would call an extended as opposed to more limited conception of academic freedom. Governments, institutions and academics tend to subscribe to one or other of these conceptions.

The second dimension is about how academics see their role in terms of academic duty. Some are focused almost exclusively at the level of the discipline or profession. Indeed, this is probably the predominant means by which academics discharge their academic duties as mentors to less experienced colleagues, as guardians of academic standards, as enablers by providing access to networks and resources, and as ambassadors for their institutions or disciplines. The identity of most academics is closely connected with their discipline, and one might expect that this would be the most common orientation. Others though relate more closely to contexts beyond the discipline or institution, especially, but not exclusively, if they work in an applied discipline or profession. These academics are concerned with serving wider society through their activities, or see their academic duty in terms of challenging and critiquing the society in which they live, in the hope of seeing a change in attitudes or practices.

Orientations

On the basis of these two dimensions, the exercise of academic freedom and the focus of academic duty, a model of intellectual leadership emerges consisting of four possible orientations (see Figure 9.1).

Knowledge producers are motivated to pursue research within the established confines of their discipline. They are seeking to have an impact on theory and/or practice through the creation of propositional or professional knowledge, through new theories, frameworks, critiques, analyses, models and discoveries. Knowledge producers work within scholarly and professional societies, research groups and departments to deepen and extend the knowledge base. As such they are largely research oriented. While they may hold strong views in private, they do not publicly engage with issues or problems that lie outside or beyond their discipline.

Academic citizens principally look to apply their disciplinary or professional specialism for the benefit of wider public understanding. They often use innovative teaching methods, occupy significant leadership roles or engage strongly in public outreach work through a range of activities with government, non-government

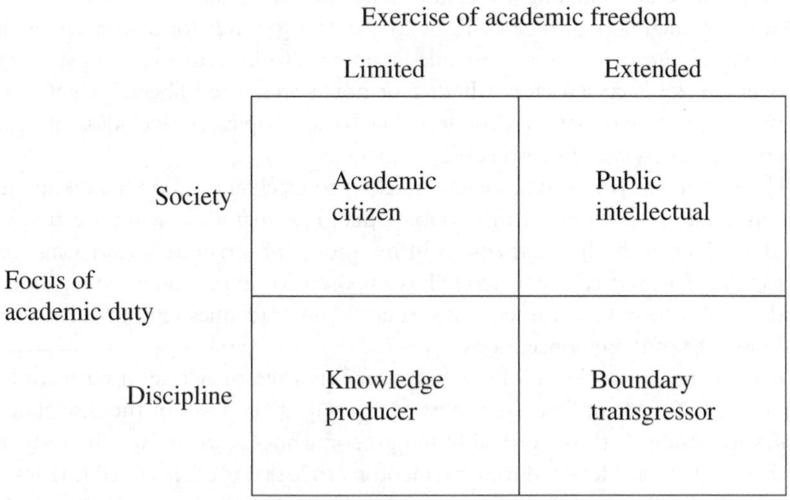

	Exercise of academic freedom	
	Limited	Extended
Society	Academic citizen	Public intellectual
Discipline	Knowledge producer	Boundary transgressor

Focus of academic duty

Figure 9.1 A model of intellectual leadership

and charitable bodies. Academic citizens see their role as confined to the application of their expertise for the benefit of society rather than engaging in areas beyond their discipline or professional boundaries. This group excludes those who engage in knowledge entrepreneurship for purely commercial gain.

Boundary transgressors seek to challenge the norms of established disciplines, and develop connections across fields of enquiry through teaching, research and scholarship. They transgress the conventional and enter into adjacent academic territories. This can include the use of methodologies that are considered radical or unconventional in the context of their discipline, publishing in journals mainly connected with other disciplines or sub-disciplines, and organizing groups, research clusters and conferences that transcend disciplinary boundaries. Boundary transgression is the means by which the map of academic knowledge is being constantly redrawn.

Public intellectuals engage with and seek to influence public debate on social, moral and economic issues through speaking, writing and campaigning. This necessitates working closely with the popular media and modern forms of communication technology. When an academic speaks out on an issue of public interest, she or he may be expressing an opinion based, to some extent, on his or her expertise but, unlike academic citizens, this is not necessarily constrained on the basis of their immediate discipline.

In relation to this model it is important to stress that orientations are not necessarily singular. Someone may be both, to some extent, a knowledge producer and an academic citizen, for example looking to apply academic knowledge in a professional or commercial context. Over the course of their career, an academic may shift orientations. Few would start out as public intellectuals but might gradually redefine their role, and see this orientation as part of their activities as they become more experienced or self-confident. Others might become frustrated or discontent with the boundaries or norms of their discipline and look to develop more interdisciplinary work, moving from an orientation as a knowledge producer to a boundary transgressor. Hence, orientations are multiple, not singular.

The following section seeks to explain these four orientations in more depth. I will illustrate them using academic obituaries taken from the UK *Times Higher Education* between 2008 and 2010. While I am associating the names of particular academics with just one orientation, it is recognized that they do commonly demonstrate characteristics associated with more than one.

Knowledge producers

Most academics, including professors, see their role as knowledge producers. In many respects this is the default orientation since it represents the natural progression from student to academic. The training received as part of a doctorate tends to encourage this primary orientation, although much will depend on the supervisor and their influence on the student. Academics want to deepen lines of conceptual and empirical enquiry. In the process they also often seek to preserve the norms and values of the discipline. They can become protective of the discipline from threats to its status and reputation. This is based on academic interests and a sense of loyalty. The seniority of full professors means that they are frequently called upon to act in ways that reinforce the boundaries of the discipline, by taking on roles such as journal reviewers and editors, chairs of conferences or scholarly societies. These roles fit the modern conception of the university professor as someone with deep personal scholarship in a subject, also willing to apply this knowledge for the benefit of society (i.e. an academic citizen). While most, if not every, academic claims to be engaged in research, this does not necessarily mean they are involved in groundbreaking or conceptually significant work. Most are making small additions to the stock of knowledge.

Knowledge production has within it two important further dimensions. It is normally thought of as being additive in the sense of trying to know more about something. But it can also be focused on trying to challenge or dislodge previous ideas, theories and understandings about the world. Here, knowledge production is concerned with being supplantive rather than just additive. Of course, researching a subject can often lead to both additive and supplantive knowledge production, since more is learnt about something and, in the process, the status of more established knowledge is challenged and possibly dislodged as a result. Hence, knowledge producers can be concerned, to some extent, with adding to the stock of knowledge without necessarily challenging established theories or practices. In this regard they may be heavily influenced or in the thrall of other academics whom they implicitly or explicitly recognize as the intellectual authorities of their field. In this sense the work of these knowledge producers is about following the lead of others. Alternatively, they can be more focused on trying to supplant existing knowledge through pursuing a more challenging research agenda that takes issue with dominant theories or practices. These are the truly original thinkers and researchers who are fewer in number. Box 9.1 gives some examples of knowledge producers.

Box 9.1 Knowledge producers

Sheila Rodwell (1947–2009) was an honorary professor of nutritional epidemiology who co-authored more than 450 publications during her career. She was credited with pioneering methods that produced more reliable data capable of measuring objective biomarkers such as urinary sugar levels in large populations. Her work led to a better understanding of the role of fat as a risk factor for a range of diseases, including breast cancer, and the benefits of eating fibre as a protective measure.

Sir James Black (1924–2010) made two significant medical discoveries that led to him being awarded the Nobel Prize for Physiology or Medicine in 1988. First his work resulted in the first beta blocker, used in the treatment of angina, heart attacks and high blood pressure. Second he developed cimetidine, which is proven to be effective in treating gastric ulcers.

Sir Clive Granger (1934–2009) collaboratively developed the concept of 'cointegration'. This concept has a range of statistical applications including demand for electricity, commodity prices and deforestation. His work won him, and Robert Engle, the Nobel Prize in 2003.

Tyrrell Burgess (1931–2009) is possibly best known for his work on polytechnics whilst working for the Higher Education Research Unit of the London School of Economics in the late 1960s. Together with John Pratt, he coined the phrase 'academic drift' to represent the way that polytechnics tended to undermine their own founding vocational rationale to ape the culture and traditions of universities in the alternate 'autonomous' tradition. He was also closely associated with the development of independent study and the pioneering of reflective statements and group work.

(Reisz 2009j, h, f, 2010a)

Knowledge producers who we recognize as intellectual leaders are engaged, intentionally or unintentionally, in the process of supplanting existing knowledge with new knowledge. The ones more likely to stand out from the pack are those capable of supplanting existing knowledge. They do more than create new knowledge. They bring about 'paradigmatic transitions wherein old paradigms are transformed in ways that result in new paradigms' (McGee Banks, 1995, p. 262). This is a process of paradigm change recognized by Kuhn (1962). This involves looking at things differently and can lead to one dominant paradigm displacing another over time.

Academic citizens

Academic citizens (Macfarlane, 2007) are those who see their role as linking their disciplinary or professional expertise with wider society through a range of activities. This might include teaching, academic leadership, outreach work, consultancy and applied forms of research. They are committed to working for the betterment of society without seeking to leverage income-generating opportunities in the process. Some may benefit materially from their work as academic citizens, receiving token payments as external examiners, for example, but they are not primarily motivated by pecuniary gain. They are willing to essentially undertake work *pro bono* in relation to their role as educators, researchers and leaders as opposed to those who engage principally in looking for ways to exploit discipline knowledge for commercial gain. This latter group of individuals might be termed knowledge entrepreneurs and need to be distinguished from academic citizens. Reputation as an intellectual leader, though, is rarely derived from commercial exploitation unless philanthropic motives are also present.

Academic citizens look to make a difference to the way in which knowledge is understood or applied. They are often looking to bring about changes in practices, policy or perhaps public perceptions. Sometimes this is via teaching activities or approaches that link theory and learning in significantly novel ways. Others may work for charitable or non-profit organizations in seeking to influence or change public perceptions connected to academic knowledge, in areas such as politics and government, public health or the alleviation of poverty (see Box 9.2 for examples). An extension of this type of work is to seek to have influence in the public policy arena, by either campaigning on particular issues or participating in policy bodies or forums. However, it needs to be understood that academic citizens, unlike public intellectuals, will not normally seek to extend their activities beyond their immediate areas of cognitive or professional expertise.

Box 9.2 Academic citizens

Ellie Scrivens (1954–2008) was a professor of health policy who successfully combined research with active engagement with healthcare providers, and was strongly committed to improving the quality of provision. She established the National Health Service Controls Assurance Support Unit, later renamed as the Health Care Standards Unit. Professor Scrivens also served as Chair of a strategic health authority and was later a non-executive director of a Primary Care Trust.

Chris Lamb (1950–2009) was a leading plant scientist, who was a vocal campaigner for plant science and was concerned that academics should obtain public trust for their work. This was connected to his commitment that his discipline could help in the struggle to address food shortages worldwide. He spoke out in favour of the commercial exploitation of genetically modified maize, despite the intimidating nature of some of the protests that took place during the mid 2000s.

Neil MacCormick (1941–2009) was both a legal expert and a campaigner for Scottish independence. He gained the prestigious Regius Professorship in public law at the University of Edinburgh when still just 31. As a Scottish nationalist he stood on five occasions, eventually becoming a Member of the European Parliament (MEP) in 1999. He used his legal expertise to noted effect as an MEP. He was a vice president of the Scottish National Party (SNP) and a special advisor to SNP leader Alex Salmond in his position as First Minister for Scotland.

John Golby (1935–2009) was a historian of popular culture who, as an early member of the history department at the UK Open University, brought together the use of tutorials, television programmes and correspondence courses. This approach laid the foundations for what is now sometimes termed 'blended' learning, where face-to-face contact with students is combined with online elements.

(Reisz 2009c, e, k, l)

Better known academic citizens appear in the media, presenting programmes that are intended to both entertain and educate. A small minority of academics are media stars, able to combine a gift for communication with the right personality and appearance to bring an academic subject to life. Examples of academics who fulfil this role include the physicist (and former pop star) Brian Cox, the archaeologist Mick Aston and the historian Simon Schama. The academic titles of some of these media stars reflects their role as professors focused on improving public understanding of their discipline. In the UK there are professors for the public understanding of science (at Oxford), risk (at Cambridge) and psychology (at Hertfordshire). The challenge they face is to balance the need to compress and, to some extent, simplify complex knowledge for a popular understanding whilst retaining academic accuracy.

While media stars bring welcome publicity to their institutions, being an academic citizen does not normally generate additional income, or significant reputational impact, for the university. This role does not fit that comfortably with academic capitalism, a concept associated with market and market-like activities, the generation of revenue by the university and the blurring of boundaries between states, markets and higher education (Slaughter and Rhoades, 2004). It represents a shift in the perceived role of the university, from the pursuit of the public good to one concerned with the demands of the market and the production of academic capitalist knowledge (Slaughter and Rhoades, 2004). At the level of the individual academic it means that an ethos of enterprise is now firmly established, 'whereby institutions are expected to foster activities of which the prime aim is to generate income' (Whitchurch and Gordon, 2010, p. 131).

One of the effects of academic capitalism on the role of the academic, and by extension the full professor, has been to bring about a shift in values at the department level, leading to the emergence of an 'entrepreneurial conception of academe' (Slaughter and Rhoades, 2004, p. 197). In my survey of professors possibly one of the most notable findings was the perception that what the university wants from professors is income generation (see Chapter 5 and 6). This is indicative of the way that universities now see professors as both knowledge producers *and* knowledge entrepreneurs. The broader orientation of being an academic citizen less easily translates into income generation.

Boundary transgressors

Espousing the importance of interdisciplinarity is a familiar mantra, a term used almost interchangeably with transdisciplinarity. Interdisciplinarity is meant to be about more than simply combining the perspectives of several disciplines (through 'multi' disciplinarity) and to involve generating new ideas, approaches and academic territories, often in relation to emerging problems or issues facing the world. Boundary transgression is critical to the process of disciplinary renewal and evolution. As such, interdisciplinarity is nothing new. The roots of biochemistry, for example, which focuses on the study of living things using chemical processes, can be traced back well over 100 years. Frederick Gowland-Hopkins, generally credited as the founding father of this interdisciplinary field, was appointed as the first professor of biochemistry at Cambridge in 1914. Transdisciplinary art provides a further example that uses a very wide range of artistic techniques and tools as a means to explore humanitarian issues. Institutions can often be keen to promote the crossing of discipline boundaries, as this can free up academic structures so often hidebound by disciplinary groupings. It is further a means of encouraging links, not just between disciplines, but also between academe and the commercial environment.

Despite rhetoric, however, the incentives for boundary transgressors in academic life are limited and possibly in decline. Interdisciplinarity is also notoriously difficult to achieve in practice. Cognitive border controls can be tight, especially when disciplines are associated with a convergent academic community (Becher, 1989). These are academic communities where the tenets and traditions of the discipline are well established, and breaching such norms will generally meet with considerable open and passive resistance. Boundaries surrounding divergent academic communities, by contrast, such as business and management studies, tend to be more permeable and less hostile to 'tourists' or 'migrants' from neighbouring fields. Research audit via peer review favours established disciplines and sub-disciplines, rather than individuals breaking out of established parameters to form new clusters and groupings. These exercises have the effect of closing down intellectual space (Barnett, 2005).

The emphasis now placed on citation scores is a further disincentive for boundary transgressors, since there are likely to be fewer colleagues willing to cite their work if they produce publications that transcend or defy conventional academic territories. Simply getting published may also be more difficult for boundary transgressors, as reviewers, protective of established academic territories, may be reluctant to allow boundary crossers to enter a different discipline field or sub-field.

Despite these challenges, however, boundary transgression is a strong feature of the intellectual leadership offered by many professors who have frequently helped to define or redefine the parameters of their disciplines and their interrelationship with others. New research centres often represent attempts to transcend or cross disciplinary boundaries. The Centre for Neuroethics at Oxford University, founded in 2009, is a good example. This centre has brought together ethicists, philosophers, neurologists, psychiatrists and legal experts in the new emerging discipline of neuroethics. Academic careers can also be illustrative of boundary transgression beyond the examples given in Box 9.3, where individuals do not just transgress but transfer across cognitive fields altogether. Lewis Elton, for example, was a professor of physics who developed an interest in the field of teaching and learning research during the 1960s, and later enjoyed great success in a second career as a professor of higher education.

Box 9.3 Boundary transgressors

Caroline Thomas (1959–2008) sought to redefine the meaning of 'security' beyond conventional understanding of this term as connected solely with military security. She broadened the conception of security to incorporate food security, access to clean water, environmental security, human rights and access to health care. Her work bridged politics and issues related to poverty. She became a professor of global politics, a title representative of the interdisciplinary nature of her scholarship. Caroline Thomas also worked as a deputy vice chancellor of the University of Southampton.

Ken Green (1946–2009) was a professor of environmental innovation management. He is credited with seeking to connect natural and social sciences through applying technology to the problems of sustainability. He pioneered a 'science and society' course as part of his commitment to an interdisciplinary approach to research and teaching. He also campaigned for changes in UK science policy.

Olivia Harris (1948–2009) was a professor of anthropology at the London School of Economics. She was noted for her wide-ranging scholarly interests, centred on making connections between anthropology and history. This was partly based on her background in history and philosophy, having read Classics. Her work bridged other academic fields and topics such as gender, feminist theory, law and work, money and motivation. Her fieldwork in South America was particularly well known in her field.

Anthony (Tony) Becher (1930–2009) was instrumental in helping to develop the field of higher education studies. Originally a mathematics and philosophy graduate, he worked as a philosopher and later for the Nuffield Foundation in developing the Cambridge Mathematics series. Becher went on to author a number of books about higher education as a professor of education at Sussex University, and is best remembered for *Academic Tribes and Territories* (1989), a groundbreaking sociological analysis of academic life.

(Reisz 2008; 2009b, d, g)

Public intellectuals

It is challenging for professors to adopt the role of a public intellectual. While this has never been easy, public intellectuals now come into conflict with the university as a corporate enterprise, more sensitive about its own image. Damage to reputation can affect the public image of an institution and, in turn, impact on student enrolment, gift giving and corporate sponsorship. Public intellectuals who criticize their own institution will tend to justify their actions on the basis of academic freedom. However, such academics may be regarded in a negative light, even by their own academic colleagues, as biting the hand that feeds. Public intellectuals more usually engage in commentary and analysis involving issues of public policy.

Despite the tradition of extramural freedom, there are many in academe and beyond who criticize those that attempt to fill the role of a public intellectual. Normally this is about their lack of perceived legitimacy in moving from their discipline into domains in which they are seen as possessing limited expert knowledge. Watson (2009) caustically remarks that academics are more certain about their views the further they are away from their true field of expertise (see Chapter 2). Johnson (1988, p. 339) is also scathing:

It is a characteristic of such intellectuals that they see no incongruity in moving from their own discipline, where they are acknowledged masters, to public affairs, where they might be supposed to have no more right to a hearing than anyone else.

Those academics committed to what C. Wright Mills would call abstract empiricism see their role as knowledge producers based on research evidence. They have little sympathy, or interest, in adopting a stance on an issue of public policy. Empiricists, focused on research evidence, can be dismissive of academics who assert their legitimacy in making value judgements. Yet, arguably, intellectual leadership demands that someone cannot 'sit on the fence' but must take a position. Burns (1978), in explaining transformational leadership (see Chapter 1), which shares many characteristics in common with intellectual leadership, has argued that moral detachment stifles intellectual creativity and is 'hostile to the concerns of the free mind' (Burns, 1978, p. 141). Public intellectuals believe that by remaining silent they are shirking a responsibility to society, and that they should use the privilege of an academic position to support a range of causes and key issues of public policy often connected with freedom and human rights. They often argue that their primary academic duty is to defend academic freedom (Thorens, 2006).

Moreover, the role of the public intellectual does not sit easily with university corporate objectives, as such activity is not associated with income generation. The need for professors to generate income, normally through research grants or via entrepreneurial activities in applying their expertise, has been stressed throughout the book. This is tied to knowledge transfer or knowledge exchange as a corporate mission. Barnett (2005, p. 109) comments that 'if one is told repeatedly that one has to generate not just one's salary but double one's salary (in order to generate the requisite institutional overheads), the space for the kind of wider civic or even oppositional function implied by the idea of "the public intellectual" is likely to close off'.

The tradition of the academic as a public intellectual is more strongly embedded in some contexts than others. It is most closely associated with the French academic tradition rather than that in Britain, for example, where it is not seen as embedded in the same way (Barnett, 2005, p. 109). While much has been written about the decline of the public intellectual (see Chapter 2), there are still influential individuals who find a way of connecting, or extending, their scholarship to reach a wider audience and address concerns of popular interest. Henry Louis 'Skip' Gates, for example, is a literary theorist and public intellectual who has argued that there is a need for a greater recognition of black literature and black culture in American education and society. As an African American himself, Gates has opposed a separatist tradition of black literature, arguing instead for the need for appropriate integration. He has also presented a number of popular television series focused on aspects of African American history and the genealogy of North Americans. This continues a tradition of public intellectuals communicating through the media to reach a wider audience, in the vein of the British historian A.J.P. Taylor.

Playing the role of the public intellectual is of particular importance in contexts where there is political repression or injustice. It is critical in the context of developing nations where academics can be comparatively more influential as among the few to speak out on such matters. For example, under Thailand's *lèse majesté* laws, those that speak out about the role of the monarchy can face a lengthy imprisonment. Academics, such as Giles Ji Ungpakorn, a professor of political science at Chulalongkorn University and author of a pro-democracy book, can find themselves charged under these laws and forced into exile (Travis, 2009). Saad Eddin Ibrahim, a former professor of sociology at the American University in Cairo, was an outspoken critic of the Egyptian president Hosni Mubarak, who was effectively deposed in 2011 at the beginning of the so-called Arab Spring. Ibrahim was arrested and imprisoned in 2000, although later released, for his opposition to the Mubarak regime and for speaking out about human rights. In South Africa, the novels of J.M. Coetzee have provided a critical commentary on the social and political conditions that existed in the apartheid era, and some of the issues that have characterized the post-apartheid period.

Conclusion

Intellectual leadership is closely connected with bringing about transformations – in developing new insights about the world, either conceptually or empirically, redrawing the boundaries of disciplines, and influencing new professional or other applied practices. It is about transforming the lives of students, fellow academics and professionals as well as members of the wider public. Not all intellectual activity is necessarily transformational. As suggested earlier in the book (see Chapter 1), intellectual leadership is closely related to the concept of transformational leadership (Burns, 1978). They both demand what I would call 'soft' characteristics associated with academic duty, or what Burns and others have labelled the giving of individualized consideration. They also require 'hard' characteristics, which I have identified as being a critic and an advocate. In short, this means having something significant to say on the basis of a critical analysis of received wisdom. In the transformational leadership literature these characteristics are about 'visioning' and 'challenging'. Both demand an ability to inspire others to follow. Yet most academics, including many professors, make relatively modest contributions in adding to our stock of knowledge or understandings about the world. Hence, it is important not to attach the label intellectual leader too readily. Nor can it be self-ascribed. This would fall into the hyperbole trap associated now with phrases like excellence and world-class (Watson, 2007). Intellectual leadership is not the norm but it does exist. It is exceptional, not common.

The model of intellectual leadership that I have presented illustrates that there are different ways of looking at this concept and giving life to it. Orientations that are based on a broader definition of academic freedom – being a public intellectual or a boundary transgressor – are generally discouraged in the corporate university environment. This is an image-conscious organization seeking to enhance its market-based reputation and generate external income, which will make it less dependent on government funding. Academics committed to these orientations of intellectual leadership are concerned with challenging the status quo, and can be seen as a reputational risk rather than as asset. Unfortunately, roles associated with a more limited view of academic freedom, notably as knowledge producer and knowledge entrepreneur, are in the ascendancy. Such dispositions fit the modern image and direction of the global university with a professoriate that serves the corporate mission. Academic productivity and entrepreneurship raises the profile and reputation of institutions without risking the controversy associated potentially with the role of professors as public intellectual, in particular. Yet the role of professors should be understood as more than knowledge producers and knowledge entrepreneurs. It is the job of professors to be the critical conscience of the profession and play a role in reminding their own institutions that this is the job of universities too.

Chapter 10

Finding a moral compass

Introduction

Earlier in the book (Chapter 4) I argued that the corporatization of the research agenda has led to universities ceding much of their responsibility for intellectual leadership. This role has been largely supplanted by economically defined measures legitimizing research activity for its functional or income generating capability. The shift in emphasis from free enquiry to an economically determined agenda lies in the way that universities now see their own identity. This has shifted from a principally curiosity-driven, independent scholarship to a service function, meeting the needs of government and industry as clients or sponsors.

In many respects, universities are in the midst of an identity crisis as a result of facing multiple demands from government, business and society. They are called upon to be efficient, business-oriented organizations, meeting the needs of a variety of stakeholders: fee-paying students increasingly aware of their rights and looking for value for money, a more highly educated and assertive generation of parents acting as co-investors in their children's education, employers looking for universities to provide graduates with industry-relevant skills, and governments demanding more efficient use of scarce public funding. In the midst of this identity crisis, public universities have been involved in activities that call into question their commitment to a just and moral society.

At the same time, as universities must satisfy the demands of their multiple stakeholders, they have another key role. This is to provide leadership on moral and intellectual issues. Here, there is a need, as I see it, for universities to balance their pursuit of income with a more explicit commitment to intellectual leadership, through championing and modelling values associated with academic freedom and democracy. One of the university's key duties is to be a 'critic and conscience of society' (Malcolm and Tarling, 2007, p. 155), and this is a role that modern institutions appear to have abandoned (Hornblow, 2007). The phrase 'critic and conscience' provides a means of understanding what it means for a university to offer intellectual leadership linked, as at the individual level, to the twin concepts of academic freedom and academic duty.

In this chapter I will explore what this implies for the university and how it can renew its commitment to this role. In doing so, I will draw on an ethical algorithm developed by Thomas Donaldson (1989) for determining whether business organizations should undertake international business dealings in foreign countries. I will suggest that this algorithm might be used as a moral compass in guiding the decision making of universities when deciding whether or not to establish links, or perhaps overseas campuses, abroad. While universities are not, by and large, perceived as business organizations, their activities increasingly resemble that of a commercial enterprise. They seek to attract fee-paying students, close courses and academic departments that are uneconomic, look for new market opportunities on a global basis and seek to exploit their intellectual capital. There are large numbers of private universities and publicly funded institutions that are seeking to diversify their income and become less dependent on state funding.

The gold rush

With confusion about their own identity and the demands they face from stake-holders, it is hardly surprising that some universities have lost their moral compass. There used to be a clear distinction between publicly and privately funded universities. Gradually though this dichotomy is eroding. Many public universities now derive more than half of their income from private sources of finance, such as alumni giving, investments and the exploitation of intellectual property. The University of Hong Kong, for example, gets only around 60 per cent of its income from the government. The remaining 40 per cent comes from tuition fees, various grants and investment income. King's College in London is typical among the elite British public universities in getting less than half its income from the government (King's College London, 2011).

This trend is partly connected with the way that government funding of higher education is now spread more thinly, as the participation rate and the number of universities has increased. There are more students and more universities but comparatively less public funding to go around. Universities need to do more with less, and therefore look to generate a higher percentage of their income from private sources. At the same time, private universities, both not-for-profit institutions with civic and religious missions and the for-profit sector, exemplified by the University of Phoenix, have expanded to capitalize on the additional demand for higher education. Rules on the funding of higher education have been relaxed or are in the process of being reformed in many countries, so that private providers can now benefit from state support, either directly or indirectly via subsidized student grants or loans. The consequence of this is that the nature of what a university is has blurred along with the division between private and public.

The blurring of the distinction between private and public is not just affecting universities. It is also affecting business organizations and their employees. The rise of corporate social responsibility means that the ethical reputation of commercial enterprises is under constant scrutiny. It is no longer acceptable to claim, as Milton Friedman did 40 years ago, that the only social responsibility of a business organization is to increase its profit for the benefit of shareholders (Friedman, 1970). Now the actions of commercial enterprises are being evaluated with regard to, among other things, their impact on the environment and the extent to which they promote equality and diversity in the workplace. The power of the internet to turn an incident viral is fuzzying the distinction between the activities of employees within and beyond the workplace, and making alleged indiscretions of various kinds harder to contain. The decision of the French fashion house Christian Dior to sack their chief designer after he was caught on film shouting anti-semitic abuse in a bar in 2011 is a case in point. Now, both universities and private companies are being judged in the court of public opinion. Reputation matters.

Hence, public universities are being pushed to become more commercial and business minded, but they find themselves caught between trying to be street-smart wheeler-dealers and upholding high standards of public and ethical conduct. In recent years this role conflict has produced a series of ethical scandals. During the political and social unrest that occurred in the Middle East in 2010, a storm of public criticism engulfed the London School of Economics (LSE) after it was found to have accepted a £1.5 million (US$2.4 million) pledge from a charity run by a son of then Libyan leader Colonel Muammar Gaddafi. LSE Director Howard Davies accepted responsibility and resigned. Cambridge University's deputy vice-chancellor also came in for criticism for being part of a delegation to the Middle East that included representatives of British arms manufacturers. Other universities in France and the United States have helped to train Libyan diplomats. But the LSE affair is only the latest in a long line of ethical controversies that have affected universities. Back in 2000, in what some saw as the ultimate irony in university corporate sponsorship, the University of Nottingham accepted £3.8 million from British American Tobacco to establish an International Centre for Corporate Social Responsibility.

The expansion of private universities increases the pressure on publicly funded institutions. Universities cannot be all things to all people. As public universities evolve by stealth into private ones, the standards and principles we expect from higher education will come under increasing pressure. The problem lies in the way that the modern university purports to be all things to all people. This is represented in the vacuity of mission statements that proclaim a commitment to a bewildering variety of stakeholders. The essential tension in the university is between two competing sets of values. One holds that the pursuit of excellence, defined in terms of scientific and scholarly achievement, is what the university should primarily be about, while the other regards equity, in relation to equality of access and opportunity for previously disadvantaged groups, as the primary goal (Trow, 2010c). The expansion of higher education over the last 30 years has thrown this tension into even sharper relief. There has been a significant expansion in participation rates on a global basis, but the growth of higher education has been accompanied by accelerated institutional differentiation between the research elite and those unable to compete on this basis. Western societies still largely expect the university to live up to its old role as a trustworthy bastion of scholarly values, yet at the same time it must also be a street-smart entrepreneur alert to every money-making opportunity. The result is that the university is forced to be Janus-faced: business facing and public spirited. While this combination of economic efficiency and social responsibility might sound laudable in practice it is hard to achieve. When compromises occur it is normally economic efficiency that wins out.

There have been nascent attempts by universities to develop policies on ethics. Yet these tend to be framed in terms that provide little guidance when doing business on an international basis, beyond abiding by the law or 'respecting the culture' of the host country. The following excerpt from an illustrative ethics code for universities produced by the UK-based Council for Industry and Higher Education gives a green light to such an essentially value-free approach:

> The institution commits itself to obeying the law and to operating in the spirit of the law by seeking to contribute to the economic well-being and social development of the countries or communities in which it operates.
>
> (CIHE, 2005a, p. 6)

While it is relatively easy to exclude doing business with or investing in certain types of organizations, such as tobacco companies and arms manufacturers, it is arguably a lot trickier to decide which countries are off limits. It is not simply a question of which countries are democratic and which are not. There has been considerable recent investment by Western universities in parts of Asia, notably China, and the Middle East. Universities have set up campuses in these rapidly developing parts of the world, eyeing an opportunity to cash in on a rapid expansion of demand for higher education.

In 2006 the University of Nottingham opened a campus in Ningbo, China with approval from the Chinese Ministry of Education. In 2010 New York University opened its Abu Dhabi campus in the United Arab Emirates. George Mason, a public US university, has been in Ras al Khaymah, one of the other emirates, since 2005. New York University also has a campus in Shanghai. Yale has numerous collaborations with Chinese universities and is opening a US style liberal arts college in collaboration with the National University of Singapore. Many other US, British and Australian universities, in particular, are involved in a range of international collaborations, involving the establishment of courses and campuses in parts of Asia and the Middle East in countries associated with dictatorial and undemocratic regimes and human rights abuses. This activity is tantamount to a 'gold rush' (Ross, 2011). In a statement about the risks inherent in this rapid expansion of higher education into parts of the world without an embedded democratic tradition or academic freedom, the American Association of University Professors offered the following warning:

> As the U.S. and Canadian presence in higher education grows in countries marked by authoritarian rule, basic principles of academic freedom, collegial

governance, and nondiscrimination are less likely to be observed. In a host environment where free speech is constrained, if not proscribed, faculty will censor themselves, and the cause of authentic liberal education, to the extent it can exist in such situations, will suffer.

(AAUP, 2009)

It also needs to be borne in mind that developing contexts do not necessarily share a Western perspective on the role of universities as founded on a public service ethic. The role of the market in higher education and as a tool for economic development has become a predominant narrative. The rationale for the growth of institutions in some developing contexts tends to be articulated in such terms, rather than necessarily serving as beacons for public service and as a critical conscience for intellectual leadership.

An ethical algorithm

University ethics policies are often narrowly construed around research ethics and issues affecting employees, such as sexual and racial equality, harassment and conflicts of interest. The word ethics seems to have become curiously, and misleadingly, synonymous with ethics in research. In a survey of UK universities, the majority of institutions declared that they did not have any other documents pertaining to ethics aside from a research ethics code (CIHE, 2005b). The survey also found that while 78 per cent of universities had an ethics committee, 'at least 61 percent of these committees were specifically for research ethics' (CIHE, 2005b, p. 33). Just seven institutions, out of around 100 in the survey, had a more general ethics or business conduct policy that was not exclusively about research ethics. This means that most universities have given little formal consideration to wider ethical issues involving corporate sponsorship, foreign investment and doing business abroad. This includes sponsorship of university research by pharmaceutical companies, which can gag academics from publishing results in a timely fashion for the common advancement of science.

The easy option is to hide behind the blanket excuse of cultural relativism and simply hope that nothing embarrassing will occur. Western universities have sometimes claimed that they have been able to reach an agreement with governments that guarantees academic freedom for faculty working at these franchise campuses. New York University Abu Dhabi, for example, claimed to have reached agreement with the authorities to create a 'cultural zone' of protected speech and conduct around the new campus, a promise that was later retracted (Ross, 2011). However, even if such a cultural zone can be agreed upon it is essentially a bubble-wrap approach, which does not extend to extramural academic freedom or provide protection for local faculty members or students. It does little, in other words, to change the prevailing culture where this involves repression of political views or the absence of democratic safeguards for ordinary citizens.

In considering their moral responsibilities, universities could do worse than to apply an ethical algorithm designed by Thomas Donaldson, a widely respected writer on the ethics of international business (Donaldson, 1989). While universities do not like to present themselves as business organizations, many operate in ways that are not dissimilar in competing with rivals, developing new markets and seeking to generate fresh income streams. Donaldson argues that organizations that do business in countries other than their own need to analyse conflicts between the norms of the 'home' country and those of the 'host' country. The home country refers to the country from which the organization that is investing or seeking to do business is based. The host country is the one in which the organization is planning to invest.

If a conflict exists between the home and the host country, the first question that needs to be asked is whether the moral reasons underlying the practice of the host country relates to its relative level of economic development. In other words, if the host country were more economically developed, would the practice probably no longer exist? An example might be levels of permitted pollution associated with manufacturing processes. When Britain and the United States were developing their industrial capacity, these countries also permitted levels of pollution that subsequently, as a result of development, were seen as unacceptable to those countries' norms. Regulations gradually reduced pollution levels. Hence, this difference is about the level of economic development rather than something embedded in a country's culture. Donaldson calls this a type 1 conflict.

An example of a type 1 conflict in relation to higher education might be where, in a host country, the percentage of young people entering university is very low, as might be found currently in a number of African or some Asian nations. A shortage of funding for economic development more generally means that participation levels are nowhere near those in many Western countries. In South Africa, the government aims to increase the participation rate in public higher education to 20 per cent by 2015. Yet in Britain, for example, the proportion of young people attending university was similarly very low, with only around 6 per cent attending in 1962. Even by the mid 1980s the participation figure was as little as 15 per cent before a further expansion took place. Hence, where a host country has a low participation rate and, in effect, an elite system of higher education, this is essentially a type 1 conflict. The moral reasons underlying the conflict with the home country are connected with its relative level of economic development.

Donaldson also identifies what he calls a type 2 conflict. This is where 'the moral reasons underlying the host country's view that the practice is permissible are independent of the host country's relative level of economic development' (Donaldson, 1989, p. 102). If such a conflict arises, an organization needs to ask itself two further questions:

- Is it possible to conduct business successfully in the host country without undertaking the practice?
- Is the practice a clear violation of a fundamental international right?

(Donaldson, 1989, p. 104)

If the answer to either one of these questions is yes, then Donaldson asserts the practice is not permissible. If a host country is engaged in a clear violation of international (human) rights, such as arresting, prosecuting and possibly executing its own citizens without trial, then this would appear to be a clear violation. However, ethical challenges for universities lie well beyond countries with high-profile reputations as human rights abusers. The difficulty, of course, comes in determining how to interpret the answer to the first question. In apartheid South Africa, many business organizations argued that they were able to operate in the country without entering into the discriminatory practices prevalent at the time. In other words, they contended that they were able to provide a separate environment in which discrimination did not occur. How far is it possible for an organization not to give succor to practices that conflict with international rights simply by their presence? In apartheid South Africa, was it genuinely possible for organizations not to enter into the practice (of racial discrimination) indirectly, by providing job opportunities at a high level for those with the best qualifications, who were predominantly members of the minority white population?

A similar difficulty arises in thinking about a country such as Malaysia. Several Australian and British universities, for example, are heavily involved in higher education in Malaysia. Both Monash University and the University of Nottingham have campuses there. Malaysia might be a moderate Islamic country with a democratic system of government, but for over 40 years it has had a policy that provides for the preferential treatment of the majority Malay population. This means that nearly all public servants, police and army recruits are Malays, who also receive housing discounts, virtually all government contracts and preferential access to universities. This is why for years Malaysian Chinese students have been forced to go abroad to get a university education. Even though ethnic Chinese and Indians have been in Malaysia for centuries, they are not treated as indigenous 'sons of the soil' or *Bumiputras*.

One way of looking at this policy is that it provides affirmative action to redress historic patterns of inequality. A less charitable interpretation is that it is an open form of racism against Malaysians of Chinese and Indian descent, who make up around one-third of the population (Hashim and Mahpuz, 2011). Whereas it is possible to find many affirmative action programmes in other countries for minorities, in Malaysia this benefits the majority over the ethnic minorities. Malaysia, though, is just one of several countries that might be criticized as having a less than desirable policy that presents an ethical question for anyone wishing to do business there.

Those universities that have chosen to establish programmes or campuses in Saudi Arabia, for example, might contend that they are able to give opportunities to both men and women in a part of the world that is rapidly developing. A less charitable interpretation is that they are looking to capitalize on an emerging market with insufficient thought to issues of fundamental human rights. Here, though, there is a challenge in determining whether the position of women in

Saudi society, which precludes co-education with men among other restrictions, is based on an amorphous definition of culture or is related to the denial of a basic international human right.

Hence, if the practice is independent of a country's level of economic development, can the university, in good conscience, do business without entering into this practice themselves or in some sense condoning it? Is the practice a fundamental breach of human rights anyway? If the answer to the first question is no, or yes to the second question, then they ought to think hard before proceeding further. The cases of Malaysia and Saudi Arabia show that there is no easy way to answer these questions. To some extent universities, like any other organization, can argue that they are not condoning or entering directly into certain practices that exist in these host countries. On the other hand, it could be argued that their mere presence legitimizes these practices.

An argument that is sometimes made is that development needs to precede democracy, and that it is unrealistic and culturally arrogant to expect otherwise. This is underpinned by a pragmatism expressed by former Malaysian Prime Minister Mahatir Mohammed, when he stated that 'you must eat before you can vote' (Kwa, 1993, p. 28). A number of high-performing Asian countries, such as Singapore, have been referred to as 'development dictatorships' (Osinbajo and Ajayi, 1994), characterized by being able to bring about economic growth through a mix of state and market-based policies, whilst maintaining tight state control over the media and continuing to place restrictions on freedom of speech. This means that the level of a country's economic development is not necessarily a barometer of the extent to which international human rights are protected.

Donaldson's algorithm provides universities with a framework for considering investment decisions before getting involved with countries where they plan to do business. Ultimately, as I have argued, they cannot be all things to all people. Universities have to draw the line in the sand somewhere if they are to continue to be respected and trusted as organizations of special character. While Donaldson (1989, p. 103) expresses the dilemma for a multinational, the same challenge exists for a university:

> A multinational must forgo the temptation to remake all societies in the image of its home society, while at the same time it must reject a relativism that conveniently forgets ethics when the payoff is sufficient.

Nearly all universities have an ethics policy, but on closer inspection the majority of these tend to be focused almost exclusively on the responsibilities of academic faculty with regard to research ethics. Here, there is a concern to ensure that research does not breach internationally recognized guidelines on the treatment of human subjects. As I have argued elsewhere, this is in many respects a limited view of research ethics, which fails to take into account other aspects of what it means to be ethical, such as authorial credit (Macfarlane, 2009). It is also important to recognize that these policies are about reputation management and minimizing the risk of litigation. They are not about the university declaring its commitment to principles or ideals that it has thought through as an organization. It is about pragmatism rather than idealism.

Reconnecting

At an individual level, the gold rush is having an impact on the way academics are being encouraged to see their role as educators. I have focused mainly on the way universities have developed a presence overseas with foreign campuses and collaborative programmes. Part of this gold rush is about the way universities now seek to attract and educate overseas students to their home country campus(es). This is also part of the drive to become more international or global in image. It is further connected to the need to diversify income streams, ensuring that in a massified higher education, with declining government funding per student, universities can find new ways of meeting their costs. As the following quotation illustrates, universities are not always keen to encourage discussion of some of the ethical issues attached to this trend:

> At a recent meeting of the faculty of which I am a member, called to discuss curriculum developments, the dean of the faculty stressed the need to develop courses that would attract overseas and local fee-paying students since university finances depended upon expanding those numbers. I responded with a speech in which I suggested that in a world beset with environmental problems, political conflicts, and the *clash of civilizations* it might be important to prepare students for leadership roles that would be sensitive to the needs of others and to the demands of cultural tolerance. The dean replied that the university is not funded for that.
>
> (Van Hooft, 2009, p. 86)

Here there is a need for the university to think more broadly about its ethical responsibilities. This is to some extent about considering more carefully who the university does business with. It is also about thinking through their responsibilities towards international students. Ensuring that there is adequate support and guidance for students from overseas is a basic requirement, but beyond this institutions need to consider issues of integration. Are international students going to be taught in classes segregated from the local or home students? If this is the case, how can this division be justified on social and moral grounds? Responsibility in marketing is another issue. Aside from ensuring that the activities are grounded in the truth rather than an attempt to deceive, a pertinent issue for universities is to ensure that the students they attract have a realistic opportunity to succeed. This means making promises they can keep in terms of support services for students with particular learning needs. While the notion that 'all can succeed' is an attractive strapline, unless universities follow through in providing a suitably supportive environment for students in practice, this claim is little more than empty marketing puff. Universities need to show moral leadership in developing marketing relationships based on trust, integrity, fairness and empathy, rather than reflecting a set of norms and practices disconnected from their own values (Gibbs and Murphy, 2009).

Conclusion

The role of the university as a contributor to economic wellbeing and development is in the ascendant. Here, institutions of higher education can play a significant role in helping to develop human capital, and provide the basis for sustained economic prosperity. However, a university is also about something else. That something else is about civic and community development. The university is not just a producer of new knowledge, but also an entity capable of offering moral leadership. It follows that faculty members, especially but not exclusively professors, need to be encouraged to see their role as public intellectuals rather than just academic capitalists. However, it is doubtful whether academics working at the micro-level will see their role in these terms, unless institutions set a good example at the macro-level.

Chapter 11

Reclaiming professorial leadership

Introduction

This final chapter takes the form of a series of recommendations aimed at senior university management. It suggests that there are ways of reclaiming the role of professors as leaders. What I mean by reclaiming is to define the role of a professor in a clearer way than it has been before. This is necessary partly due to the expansion of higher education on a global basis, which has brought with it an expansion of the professoriate. It is also necessary as the nature of higher education itself has changed. Throughout the book I have argued that being a professor should be about:

- balancing the privileges of academic freedom with the responsibilities of academic duty;
- carrying out a role or roles as an intellectual leader of some kind expressed as knowledge producer, academic citizen, boundary transgressor and public intellectual.

My first point implies that professors need to have an all-round commitment, both to their own teaching and scholarship and to the development of others, including their own institution. This does not preclude the disaggregation of the professorial role into specialist tracks, but it means that even research professors need to engage in work as a responsible academic citizen. Being a professor, in other words, should not be seen as a licence to be selfish. There are collegial duties that are essential to the future of a healthy, productive and influential academic profession.

Universities also need to think of professors as more than strong researchers (the research professor) or academic managers (the managerial professor). I have proposed a series of orientations (i.e. knowledge producer, academic citizen, boundary transgressor and public intellectual) that go beyond functional roles. Currently universities tend to characterize the professorial role mainly in terms of either being a researcher or a manager. This has had a divisive and dichotomizing effect on higher education. It also misrepresents the variety and range of ways in which professors can be intellectual leaders within and beyond the institution. This does not mean to imply that research and academic management are unimportant. What I mean is that professors can achieve more as intellectual leaders in a broader sense. Often these things are being achieved but they are rarely articulated.

What is required is a reevaluation of what is expected of professors, and a commitment on behalf of institutions to look at their needs and their role differently. Part of this is about developing professors for and in their role, incentivizing them to regard this position as a new start rather than end point of their academic career, and ensuring that their local as well as cosmopolitan role is encouraged and rewarded. The ideal professor is a 'rooted cosmopolitan' (Nixon, 2010b).

What follows are my suggestions for achieving these goals.

1. Induct and develop professors

It sounds all too obvious. Yet it needs to be said. Professors, especially new ones, like anybody else, need guidance and development in order to better succeed in their role. My research into this subject reveals that there is very little of any such provision currently available. Other researchers also agree that expectations are too often implied rather than stated explicitly (Rayner *et al.*, 2010). The assumption is made that professors who meet the criteria for their appointment will be instantly able to perform as an intellectual leader. But are professors born rather than made? Do they possess the necessary qualities and abilities to exercise the skills associated with academic duty as well as academic freedom? The criteria for becoming a professor are essentially about individual achievement, whereas being a professor demands a more balanced set of skills and dispositions. There is little evidence to support the assumption that professors are born not made, just as there is little evidence to support the idea that someone who possesses a doctorate necessarily makes a competent teacher.

One of the key themes emerging from my survey was that professors feel there is a lack of guidance and clarity with respect to what universities want from them. They feel that universities do not make clear what the expectations of them are. The following comments are illustrative of this view:

> The university could make more structured and effective use of the leadership qualities and experience of the senior professors instead of relying on them or expecting them to define their own personal agenda all the time.
>
> (professor of history)

> I think the university is very unclear as to what it wants. It is clear in promotion panels and then fails to performance manage or monitor.
>
> (professor of health sciences)

Is there any training for profs on the leadership role? That would be great. Currently there appear to be no expectations beyond the promotion/ appointment panel.

(professor of linguistics)

Too often colleagues think it [i.e. being a professor] is about publishing more when actually the key is undertaking service which enables one to network and form social and political capital.

(professor of management)

What form might professorial leadership development take? Here, I am not suggesting lengthy compulsory courses of formally certified training and education. This is clearly impractical. But there is a case for short courses and targeted development often on a small group or individual basis. Newly appointed professors, for example, might benefit from a one-day induction into what it means to be a professor, both generically and in terms of institutional expectations, just as new groups of faculty are inducted mainly in respect to the teaching role. However, this is not intended to imply an anodyne induction into university 'processes and procedures'. It needs to engage professors to discuss how they might articulate their role. Whatever form this training might take, it is important to emphasize within it that the role extends well beyond the pursuit of a personal publication agenda, including the ability to develop mature scholarly networks. The model of intellectual leadership I present in the book (see Chapter 9) provides three alternative or, perhaps, additional orientations to the common expectation that professors should be knowledge producers and knowledge entrepreneurs.

Further, there is the need to get academics to think about intellectual leadership at an earlier point of their career. The only real training they receive to be a professor is taking a doctorate and not all professors even possess this qualification, especially those in practice-based fields. Hence, we might consider expending rather more effort on explaining to research students what intellectual leadership might mean. It is not just about writing grant applications or publishing papers, but also refers to acquiring the art of skilful and constructive peer review, widening intellectual networks, critiquing and shaping academic trends, understanding and participating in team-based interdisciplinary research, learning how to engage non-academic audiences in both research processes and the application of research outcomes, mentoring of new researchers and nurturing academic freedom.

2. Encourage horizontal (not just vertical) academic careers

Conventionally, academic careers tend to be seen in linear terms. In other words, people move from junior to more senior ranks over time, climbing up the greasy pole. You start as a 'fledgling' for the first few years, before entering into a 'maturing' phase, becoming 'established', until eventually, after around 25 years' service, turning into a 'patriarch' (Bayer and Dutton, 1977). Such categories have been used to evaluate the research performance of academics over the course of an academic career. The conclusion of this study of academic careers, though, was that across a range of disciplines 'career age (and possibly tenure status) is a poor predictor of research-professional activity' (Bayer and Dutton, 1977, p. 279). What this implies is that age categories are not as important as we might think. They indicate how much experience someone has, and possibly roughly how old they are, rather than being informative about someone's effectiveness and performance as an academic.

The default model for thinking about academic careers is still based on graduation into an academic job after the completion of a full-time doctorate. Yet this way of thinking about academic careers is very dated, given the growth of vocational subjects in universities. This means that academics are just as likely to enter a university career after a period as a practice-based professional, rather than following the completion of a doctorate. Hence, age and years in academe do not necessarily correspond. In an expanded higher education system it is not just the students who are different and more diverse. The same applies to the professoriate. A further possible assumption behind such a classification is that faculty members spend their careers largely in one institution, since becoming a patriarch may be more problematic in an institution one has just joined.

Hence, there is a need to look at academic careers differently as horizontal not just vertical paths. What this means is that academics move between a variety of roles throughout the course of their careers, which may represent moves that are sideways as well as up. As referred to earlier in the book, the academic role is unbundling or disaggregating. In an analysis of contemporary roles, an Australian study identifies seven types of modern academic. Aside from the 'classic academic' who performs teaching, research and service duties in roughly equal measure, contemporary roles include 'the engaged academic', the 'disciplinary research leader' and the 'senior academic leader' (Coates and Goedegebuure, 2010).

In practice, academics move between these various roles during the course of their careers. The same is true of professors, especially those appointed at a relatively early stage of their career. Such individuals, perhaps appointed during their early forties, may spend time initially in further building their scholarly reputation via a spell as a research professor, and a little later might take on leadership of their department or unit as well as more of a classic professor. They might then return to the role of a research professor after a few years as head of department, later becoming via the impact of their work a star professor. Alternatively, they might decide to forge a career as a managerial professor, later becoming a senior university leader, such as a dean of faculty or vice president. In other words, the career of a professor is no more linear than that of any other academic. This type of horizontal rather than linear career path is common and needs to be understood and supported by senior management.

One of the dangers of making someone a professor is that they may regard this appointment as the crowning achievement of their career. It can be a valediction for a lifetime of scholarly endeavour. As an affirmation of personal worth, being made a professor is significant, based, as it normally is, on substantial scholarly achievements over a sustained period. However, the symbolic significance of being made a professor should not overshadow the fact that it is a new beginning to another career phase rather than an end point. In the worst instances this can create the same impression as the phrase 'get tenure, stop working' (Kimball, 1990, p. xl).

Institutions tend to pay too little attention to structuring or scaffolding the careers of their professors through devising further, explicit reward and recognition criteria. Informally most institutions do have differential pay structures for professors, but this is less often made explicit or transparent or linked to job descriptions.

3. Evaluate creativity and originality, not just productivity

Per capita, professors will probably represent the most expensive intellectual resource in an institution's budget. Thus, it is not unreasonable to expect quite a bit in return from them. Contemporary institutions have tended to focus their evaluation of professors on their income-generation capacity, and the impact of their research outputs. These intellectual metrics are mainly concerned with the productivity of academics, normally, but not exclusively, in the form of refereed journal papers and the extent to which these have impact measured in terms of citations. Added to this there is also now increasing attention on the extent of impact in knowledge transfer or knowledge exchange activities.

Evaluating professors in this way may increase productivity in a narrow sense of numbers of publications, but does little to promote creativity or originality. The prescription that academics must seek to collect evidence of their impact via citations encourages safety in numbers in popular sub-disciplines, rather than striking out in a new direction away from the pack. It means that academics end up researching and writing about similar things and trying to publish in a very limited and narrow range of journals. Nor are the journals that are most highly rated necessarily the most international. Institutions are now effectively determining not only what professors should research (via research themes) but also where the results of this work should be published, in a limited number of high-impact journals (see Chapter 4). This leaves little room for the individual direction of scholarship.

The focus on metrics is discouraging professors from pursuing work that is innovative and risky. Instead, before considering the intellectual merits of a particular research path they are effectively required to consider the amount of funding a research project is likely to attract, or whether it fits into a university or government research council research theme. Some of my interviewees recognized this problem:

> My own sense is that more should be made of Universities themselves as a place of learning with the inherent aspects of 'risk' and 'experimentation' thrown in.
>
> (professor of English)

Here, there is a need for institutions to balance more carefully the need to develop and present a coherent picture of the institution's research activities as a marketing imperative, whilst developing an environment that encourages and sustains creative scholarship. Corralling professors into research clusters associated with university-level research themes does not provide an environment conductive to new, controversial and innovative thinking. Here, institutions might consider adopting a support framework around non-themed or blue skies research, as well as themed research as part of a balanced approach.

4. Treat professors as locals as well as cosmopolitans

The scenario is a familiar one. A soccer or baseball team is taken over by a billionaire having spent years in the doldrums without success in the big league. Instantly there is a cash injection. New, star players join the club attracted by lucrative contracts and the promise of enjoying an even higher status. The fans are excited as they eagerly await the club's new dawn in the hope that it will bring glory. Yet despite all the money laid out, the team fails to perform. Why? The stars do not seem that committed. There seems to be little teamwork going on. The fans fear the players have really only signed on for large paycheques in what is probably the twilight of their careers.

It would be a mistake to imagine that this scenario is limited to the world of professional sport. It is all too familiar in the world of higher education, when ambitious universities seek to boost their prestige or research ranking by recruiting star professors. Individuals recruited on the basis of their personal research reputations are not necessarily committed to the institution and in developing others within it. Simply assuming that others will be positively affected by the buzz created by such individuals overlooks what can be shortcomings in making expectations clear. In many universities there are middle-ranking academics with potential, but without mentoring support they are unlikely to break through to win major research grants or publish significant papers. They may also be lacking the access to the key networks that professors as enablers possess (see Chapter 8).

One of the cardinal errors made by universities has been to appoint star professors without making such mentoring and other forms of what I call academic citizenship (Macfarlane, 2007) clear. Star professors are, by definition, cosmopolitans (Merton, 1947). In other words, their main point of identity is outside the institution within their discipline and in international research groups and scholarly societies (Gouldner, 1957). They are leading influential figures in these contexts, boundaryless rather than boundaried by their institutional affiliation (Dowd and Kaplan, 2005). This is, after all, why they are stars. However, a university and its faculty may feel short-changed unless all professors, and not just star names, act not only as cosmopolitans but as locals (Merton, 1947) or more boundaried academics (Dowd and Kaplan, 2005). Such individuals have less commitment to specialized role skills, like research and publication, but are highly loyal to the organization and knowledgeable about how it operates (Gouldner, 1957).

In practical terms being a local means being involved in institutional affairs, serving on appropriate committees, contributing ideas internally, promoting the interests of the university as professor as ambassador (see Chapter 8) and perhaps advising senior members of university management. Allied to this it is important that professors are expected to act as mentors to less experienced faculty, and develop skills in bringing on others in their academic careers through activities like joint authorship, or in acting as a critical friend when a colleague is developing a grant proposal or a paper for publication. Much of this work is less than visible but nonetheless vitally important. Ideally a professor is a 'cosmo-local' (Goldberg, 1976) with an orientation that serves both internal university and external professional and discipline-based communities. On the basis of my survey, this is also how most professors see themselves, but feel that institutions rarely make sufficient use of their talents as a local, or place enough value on the contributions that they make in this regard (Macfarlane, 2011a).

The importance of service or academic citizenship is embedded in what it means to *be* a professor – connected with the academic duties I outline in Chapter 8 – but rarely plays a significant role in appointment decisions, particularly in a UK context. A relatively simple and practical way to increase the relative importance of academic citizenship is to divide such contributions into internal and external service. *Internal service* refers to things such as mentoring departmental colleagues, serving on university committees and project teams, leadership roles within the institution, and course management responsibilities. *External service* includes serving scholarly and professional societies as well as government, business and charitable organizations in a variety of ways, giving guest lectures, external examining and peer review work for research councils and journals among other things. Doing this rebalances appointment criteria by shifting from three categories – research, teaching and service – to four – research, teaching, internal service and external service. It also explicitly recognizes the importance of professors being good locals *and* good cosmopolitans.

If there is an expectation that professors should work as locals as well as cosmopolitans this needs to be spelt out in job descriptions. If there is no expectation that a professor will act as a local this can have an adverse impact on their relationships within the institution, and can lead to feelings of resentment and even hostility among other members of faculty, leading to caustic comments about 'air miles' professors. Hence, ensuring a balance is struck between the local and cosmopolitan role is important in aligning expectations and in integrating a new professor into an institution.

5. Make better use of emeritus professors

The population of many developed countries is ageing. Thanks to advances in medical science and higher standards of living, life expectancy continues to rise. The academic profession is also ageing (Coates *et al.*, 2010), and with the global expansion of higher education, there is a shortage in many countries of adequately trained and qualified young academics to replace those heading toward retirement. But why do professors need to retire at say 60 or 65 years of age? Many do so through choice. They have had enough of academic life and want to spend the rest of their life doing something else.

However, there are many who want to continue to teach and research. Being an academic is more than just a job; it is also a lifelong vocation. Moreover, retirement ages are a purely arbitrary restriction on the length of an academic career and an increasingly irrelevant one. As life expectancy has increased so has the length of time that someone can usefully engage in academic activities. Some of the most influential professors in the modern world are emeritus in status – the influential feminist Germaine Greer, who is professor emerita of English literature and comparative studies at the University of Warwick; the evolutionary biologist Richard Dawkins, who has developed a reputation as a critic of creationism; and Noam Chomsky, professor emeritus of linguistics at Massachusetts Institute of Technology.

There are two reasons for thinking more carefully and creatively about how emeritus professors might be more seriously engaged in working with the university in the future. One is that anti-discrimination laws are beginning to take ageism more seriously. In the UK, the law has recently changed and the mandatory retirement age has now been abolished. Since the early 1990s, there has been no official retirement age for professors in North America (Thody, 2011). The second reason for rethinking the role of emeriti is the shortage of well-qualified academic staff, and the continuing contribution that older and experienced faculty can make. The expansion of higher education on a global basis has not been accompanied by a corresponding increase in the number of qualified academics. This means that there is also a very practical reason for thinking more clearly about how the knowledge and skills of emeritus professors might be better utilized.

Offering a more organized approach to the involvement of emeritus professors is important for one further reason. This is connected with the importance of ensuring that academics at lower rank can continue to progress and are not 'blocked' by the reluctance of senior professors to retire. In some fields professorial positions are scarce, and opportunities for younger scholars to progress may be limited. If professors are unwilling to retire this may have adverse repercussions in some disciplines to the process of scholarly renewal and leadership. Here, so-called staged retirements can be linked to an eventual emeritus position, as it might otherwise be tempting for a senior professor to remain in post well past normal retirement age for reasons of academic identity, as well as for the financial rewards such a position carries.

In the United States, in particular, a number of institutions have established emeritus colleges. These are organizations, both at university and community-college level, that offer retired faculty members the opportunity to continue to contribute to educational activities. As the website of Arizona State University explains, its emeritus college exists as a means for continuing fruitful engagement with productive scientists, scholars and artists who may have retired from their faculty positions but not from their disciplines (Arizona State University, 2011). Universities in other parts of the world might usefully consider what they could learn from the emeritus college model.

6. Expect professors to be intellectual leaders

The criteria for becoming a professor are well established – publications, research grants, the impact of the scholar internationally, professional recognition and esteem indicators, and, perhaps, teaching excellence and service to the institution as well. However, these things do not speak to what an academic is expected to *be* when they become a professor. Here, the definition of four forms of intellectual leadership – knowledge producer, academic citizen, boundary transgressor and public intellectual – (see Chapter 9) might be a useful guide. A professor will probably have the capacity to offer a contribution to more than one of these forms depending on their interests and background.

Creating a divide between professors and managers is an unwise strategy. It drives a wedge between those with organizational power and those with intellectual authority. Encouraging the unbundling of the professorial role through nomenclature such as research professor or teaching and learning professor adds to this hollowing out and sense of exclusion. The evidence shows that the best university leaders are scholars (Goodall, 2009):

> Generally, those universities that have made best use of professors are those in which professors dominate the central management structure of the institution and completely permeate and purvey it at every level, because that is the way you actually really sustain a culture. ... I think you have got to have empathy from the very top right through every level.
>
> (professor of economics)

If you do not regard the professors who have been appointed in your institution as intellectual leaders, this calls into question why they were made professors in the first place. Part of the answer to this question is that the institution may have expected too little in return from those that they have appointed. Here, as I have pointed out in the book, there has been a tendency to appoint professors to fulfil a narrower role as a knowledge producer rather than contribute in other ways to the life of the institution and the betterment of society.

Conclusion

So, to summarize, my suggestions are that the professoriate is a valuable resource that needs to have its role more clearly articulated, and that individuals appointed might usefully receive some development for their new designation. In this way expectations could be made clearer and the institution would benefit from greater engagement with and value from the expertise that professors possess, treating them as locals as well as cosmopolitans. It is also important I believe to encourage professors to continue to grow as intellectual leaders through thinking through their future development, perhaps as public intellectuals and boundary transgressors, as well as in producing new knowledge and capitalizing on its market potential. Here, the social role of the professoriate needs to be balanced with its economic value. They are key individuals who act as role models for the generation of scholars that will come after them. It is in everyone's interests that more thought is given to their role as intellectual leaders.

Bibliography

Academics for Academic Freedom. (2011). *Homepage*, http://afaf.web.officelive. com/default.aspx (accessed 14 January 2011).

Altbach, P. (2006). Cosmopolitanism run amok: work and rewards in Asia's universities. In P. Altbach (Ed.), *International Higher Education: Reflections on Policy and Practice* (pp. 151–154). Boston, MA: Center for International Higher Education, Boston College.

American Association of University Professors (AAUP). (1915). *Declaration of Principles on Academic Freedom and Academic Tenure*, http://www.aaup.org/AAUP/ pubsres/policydocs/contents/1915.htm (accessed 14 November 2010).

——(2009). *On Conditions of Employment at Overseas Campuses*, http://www.aaup. org/aaup/comm/rep/a/overseas.htm (accessed 14 January 2011).

——(2011a). *Average Salaries of Full Professors, by Discipline, as a Percentage of the Average Salary of Full Professors of English Language and Literature, 1980–81 to 2009–10*, http://www.aaup.org/AAUP/comm/rep/Z/ecstatreport10–11/TOC. htm (accessed 3 June 2011).

——(2011b). *Distribution of Faculty by Rank, Gender, Category, and Affiliation, 2010–2011*, http://www.aaup.org/AAUP/comm/rep/Z/ecstatreport10–11/TOC. htm (accessed 3 June 2011).

Arizona State University (2011). *Emeritus College Homepage*, http://emerituscollege. asu.edu/ (accessed 5 July 2011).

Arnold, M. (1869). *Culture and Anarchy*. London: Smith, Elder & Co.

Arnoldi, J. (2007). Universities and the public recognition of expertise, *Minerva*, 45, 49–61.

Barnes, D.E. and Bero, L.A. (1998). Why review articles on the effects of passive smoking reach different conclusions, *Journal of the American Medical Association*, 279, 1566–1570.

Barnett, R. (1990). *The Idea of a University*. Maidenhead: Society for Research into Higher Education and Open University Press.

——(2005). Academics as intellectuals. In D. Cummings (Ed.), *The Changing Role of the Public Intellectual* (pp. 108–122). London: Routledge.

——(2003). *Beyond All Reason: Living with Ideology in the University*. Buckingham: Society for Research into Higher Education and the Open University Press.

Bassnett, S. (2004). *The Changing Role of the Professor*. National Conference of University Professors, http://www.rdg.ac.uk/ncup/Susan%20Bassnett.htm. (accessed 12 May 2009).

Bauchspies, W.K., Croissant, J. and Resturo, S. (2006). *Science, Technology and Society*. Oxford: Blackwell.

Bauman, Z. (1987). *Legislators and Interpreters: On Modernity, Post-Modernity and Intellectuals*. Cambridge: Polity Press.

Bayer, A.E. and Dutton, J.E. (1977). Career age and research-professional activities of academic scientists: tests of non-linear models for higher education faculty policies, *The Journal of Higher Education*, 48, 3, 259–282.

Becher, T. (1982). *Managing Basic Units*. Report from the Institutional Management in Higher Education Programme Special Topic Workshop held in Paris between 23 November and 1 December 1982, Paris: OECD.

——(1989). *Academic Tribes and Territories: Intellectual Enquiry and the Cultures of Disciplines*. Buckingham: Society for Research into Higher Education and the Open University Press.

Becher, T. and Kogan, M. (1992). *Process and Structure in Higher Education*. London: Routledge.

Blackmore, P. and Castley, A. (2006). *Developing Capacity in the University*. http://www.lfhe.ac.uk/networks/theme/executivebriefing.pdf (accessed 20 August 2010).

Bloom, A. (1987). *The Closing of the American Mind*. New York: Simon & Schuster.

Bolden, R., Petrov, G. and Gosling, J. (2008). *Developing Collective Leadership in Higher Education: Final Report*. London: Leadership Foundation for Higher Education.

——(2009) Distributed leadership in higher education: rhetoric and reality, *Educational Management Administration and Leadership*, 37, 2, 257–277.

Boshier, P. (2002). Farm-gate intellectuals, excellence and the university problem in Aotearoa/New Zealand, *Studies in Continuing Education*, 24, 1, 5–24.

Bourdieu, P. (1986). The forms of capital. In J. Richardson (Ed.) *Handbook of Theory and Research for the Sociology of Education* (pp. 241–258). New York: Greenwood.

——(1989) The corporatism of the universal: the role of intellectuals in the modern world, *Telos*, 81, Fall, 99–110.

——(Trans. R. Nice) (1999). *Acts of Resistance: Against the Tyranny of the Market*. New York: New Press.

Boyatzis, R.E. (1982). *The Competent Manager*. New York: John Wiley.

Boyer, E. (1990). *Scholarship Reconsidered: Priorities of the Professoriate*. Princeton, NJ: University Press.

Brennan, J. (2011). Higher education and social change: researching the 'end times'. In J. Brennan and T. Shah (Eds.) *Higher Education and Changing Times: Looking Back and Looking Forward* (pp. 6–12). London: Centre for Higher Education Research & Information, The Open University.

Bright, D. and Richards, M. (2001). *The Academic Deanship: Individual Careers and Institutional Roles*. San Francisco: Jossey-Bass.

Brock, M.G. (1996). The intellectual and the university: an historical perspective, *Reflections on Higher Education*, 8, 66–81.

Brown, A.D. and Starkey, K. (2000). Organizational identity and learning: a psychodynamic approach, *The Academy of Management Review*, 25, 1, 102–120.

Brown, D. and Gold, M. (2007). Academics on non-standard contracts in UK universities: portfolio work, choice and compulsion, *Higher Education Quarterly*, 61, 4, 439–460.

Bryman, A. (2007). Effective leadership in higher education: a literature review, *Studies in Higher Education*, 32, 6, 693–710.

Burgan, M. (2006). *Whatever Happened to the Faculty? Drift and Decision in Higher Education*. Baltimore, MD: The Johns Hopkins University Press.

Burns, J.M. (1978). *Leadership*. New York: Harper & Row.

Careers Research and Advisory Centre Limited (CRAC) (2011) *The Researcher Development Framework*. Cambridge: CRAC.

Cameron, D. (2006). *Speech*. 24 November, http://www.news.bbc.co.uk/1/hi/uk_politics/6179078.stm (accessed 15 October 2010).

Castells, M. (2000). *The Rise of the Network Society*. Oxford: Blackwell.

Coaldrake, P. (2001). Rethinking academic and university work, *Higher Education Management*, 12, 2, 7–30.

Coates, H. and Goedegebuure, L. (2010). The real academic revolution: why we need to reconceptualise Australia's future academic workforce, and eight possible strategies for how to go about this, *Research Briefing*. Melbourne: LH Martin Institute.

Coates, H., Dobson, I.R., Goedegebuure, L. and Meek, L. (2010). Across the great divide: what do Australian academics think of university leadership? Advice from the CAP Survey, *Journal of Higher Education Policy and Management*, 32, 4, 379–387.

Cohen, S. (1972). *Folk Devils and Moral Panics: The Creation of the Mods and Rockers*. Oxford: Basil Blackwell.

Coleman, J.S. (1977). The academic freedom and responsibilities of foreign scholars in African universities, *ISSUE: A Quarterly Journal of African Opinion*, 7, 2, 14–32.

Committee of Vice Chancellors and Principals (CVCP) (1985). Report of a Steering Committee for Efficiency Studies in Universities (*The Jarratt Report*). London: CVCP.

Council for Industry and Higher Education (CIHE) (2005a). *Ethics and the University*, http://www.cihe.co.uk/category/knowledge/publications/ (accessed 26 May 2011).

——(2005b). *Ethics Matters: Managing Ethical Issues in Higher Education*, http://www.cihe.co.uk/category/knowledge/publications/ (accessed 26 May 2011).

Conroy, J.P. (2000). *Intellectual Leadership in Education*. Dordrecht: Kluwer.

Cousin, G. (2011). Rethinking the concept of 'Western', *Higher Education Research and Development*, 30, 5, 585–594.

Cummings, D. (1998). The service university in comparative perspective, *Higher Education*, 35, 1–8.

——(2005). Introduction: ideas, intellectuals and the public. In D. Cummings (Ed.) *The Changing Role of the Public Intellectual* (pp. 1–7). London: Routledge.

Currie, J., Petersen, C.J. and Mok, K.H. (2006) *Academic Freedom in Hong Kong*. Oxford: Lexington Books.

Dawkins, R. (1976). *The Selfish Gene*. Oxford: Oxford University Press.

——(2006). *The God Delusion*. New York: Bantam Press.

Deem, R. and Brehony, K.J. (2005). Management as ideology: the case of 'New Managerialism' in higher education, *Oxford Review of Education*, 31, 2, 217–235.

Department of Health and Social Security (1980). *Inequalities in Health: Report of a Research Working Group. 'The Black Report'*. London: DHSS.

Donaldson, T. (1989). *The Ethics of International Business*. Oxford: Oxford University Press.

Dopson, S. and McNay, I. (1996). Organizational culture. In D. Warner and D. Palfreyman (Eds.), *Higher Education Management* (pp. 16–32). Buckingham: Society for Research into Higher Education and Open University Press.

Dowd, K.O. and Kaplan, D.M. (2005). The career life of academics: boundaried or boundaryless? *Human Relations*, 58, 6, 699–721.

Drake, D. (2005). *French Intellectuals and Politics from the Dreyfus Affair to the Occupation*. New York: Palgrave Macmillan.

Eagleton, T. (2006). Lunging, flailing, mispunching: review of *The God Delusion* by Richard Dawkins, *London Review of Books*, 28, 20, 32–34.

Ecclestone, K. and Hayes, D. (2009). Changing the subject: educational implications of emotional well-being, *Oxford Review of Education*, 35, 3, 371–389.

Edgerton D. (2009). The Haldane principle and other invented traditions in science policy, *History and Policy*, 88, http://www.historyandpolicy.org/papers/policy-paper-88.html (accessed 26 June 2011).

Etzkowitz, H. and Leydesdorff, L. (2000). The dynamics of innovation: from national systems and 'Mode 2' to a triple helix of university–industry–government relations, *Research Policy*, 29, 2, 109–123.

Feldman, K.A. and Paulsen, M.B. (1999). Faculty motivation: the role of a supportive teaching culture, *New Directions in Teaching and Learning*, 78, 71–78.

Finkelstein, M.J. and Schuster, J.H. (2001). Assessing the silent revolution: how changing demographics are reshaping the academic profession, *American Association of Higher Education Bulletin*, 54, 2, 3–7.

Fox, K. (2004). *Watching the English: The Hidden Rules of English Behaviour*. London: Hodder & Stoughton.

Friedman, M. (1970). The social responsibility of business is to increase its profits, *New York Times Magazine*, 13 September.

Fuller, S. (2005). *The Intellectual*. London: Icon Books.

Furedi, F. (2004). *Where Have All The Intellectuals Gone? Confronting 21st Century Philistinism*. London: Continuum.

Froggatt, P. (1992). Obituary: Eric Ashby, *The Independent*, 28 October, http://www.independent.co.uk/news/people/obituary-lord-ashby-1559996.html (accessed 2 February 2011).

Gibbons, M., Limoges, C., Nowotny, H., Schwartzman, S., Scott, P. and Trow, M. (1994). *The New Production of Knowledge: The Dynamics of Science and Research in Contemporary Societies*, London: Sage.

Gibbs, P. and Murphy, P. (2009). Implementation of ethical higher education marketing, *Tertiary Education and Management*, 15, 4, 341–354.

Goldberg, A.I. (1976). The relevance of cosmopolitan/local orientations to professional values and behavior, *Sociology of Work and Occupations*, 3, 331–356.

Goodall, A. (2009). *Socrates in the Boardroom: Why Research Universities Should Be Led by Top Scholars*. Princeton, NJ: Princeton University Press.

Gordon, G. (2005). The human dimensions of the research agenda, *Higher Education Quarterly*, 59, 1, 40–55.

Gordon, L.P. (2010). The market colonization of intellectuals, *Truthout*, 6 April, http://www.truth-out.org/the-market-colonization-intellectuals58310 (accessed 6 February 2011).

Gordon, P.E. (2009). *What is Intellectual History? A Frankly Partisan Introduction to a Frequently Misunderstood Field*, http://history.fas.harvard.edu/

people/faculty/documents/pgordon-whatisintellhist.pdf (accessed 6 December 2010).

Gossop, M. and Hall, W. (2009). Clashes between government and its expert advisers, *British Medical Journal*, 339, 4662.

Gouldner, A.W. (1957). Cosmopolitans and locals: toward an analysis of latent social roles – I, *Administrative Science Quarterly*, 2, 3, 281–306.

Grant, K.R. and Drakich, J. (2010). The Canada Research Chairs Program: the good, the bad, and the ugly, *Higher Education*, 59, 21–42.

Greer, G. (1970). *The Female Eunuch*. London: Verso.

Gumport, P. (2002). *Academic Pathfinders: Knowledge Creation and Feminist Scholarship*. Westport, CT: Greenwood Press.

Haldane Report (1918). *Report of the Machinery of Government Committee under the Chairmanship of Viscount Haldane of Cloan*. HMSO: London.

Halsey, A.H. (1992). An international comparison of access to higher education. In *Lessons from Cross-National Comparison of Education*, Wallingford: Triangle Books.

Halsey, A.H. and Trow, M. (1971). *The British Academics*. London: Faber & Faber.

Harloe, M. and Perry, B. (2005). Rethinking or hollowing out the university? External engagement and internal transformation in the knowledge economy, *Higher Education Management and Policy*, 17, 2, 29–41.

Harman, G. (2002). Academic leaders or corporate managers? Deans and Heads of Australian higher education, 1977 to 1997, *Higher Education Management and Policy*, 14, 53–70.

Hashim, M.A. and Mahpuz, M. (2011). Tackling multiculturalism via human communication: a public relations campaign of Malaysia, *International Journal of Business and Social Science*, 2, 4, 114–127.

Henkel, M. (2000). *Academic Identities and Policy Change in Higher Education*. London: Jessica Kingsley.

Hickson, K. (2009). Conservatism and the poor: Conservative party attitudes to poverty and inequality since the 1970s, *British Politics*, 4, 341–362.

HESA (Higher Education Statistics Agency) (2008). *Summary of Academic Staff in all UK institutions 2006/07*, http://www.hesa.ac.uk (accessed 8 November 2008).

——(2009). HESA data shows increase in proportion of female professors. *Press Release*, 30 March 2009, http://www.hesa.ac.uk/index.php/content/view/1397/161/ (accessed 9 April 2011).

——(2011). *Staff Data Tables: All Academic Staff*, http://www.hesa.ac.uk/index.php?option=com_content&task=view&id=1898&Itemid=239 (accessed 26 February 2011).

Hogg, P. (2007). On becoming and being a professor, *Synergy: Imaging and Therapy Practice*, June, 3–5.

Hornblow, D. (2007). The missing universities: absent critics and consciences of society. In *37th Conference of the Philosophy of Education Society of Australasia Inc.*, Wellington: New Zealand.

Horowitz, I.L. (Ed.) (1963). *Power, Politics and People: The Collected Essays of C. Wright Mills*. Oxford University Press: New York.

Jacoby, R. (1987). *The Last Intellectuals: American Culture in the Age of Academe*, New York: Basic Books.

Johnson, P. (1988). *Intellectuals*. London: Phoenix Press.

Jump, P. (2011). Delete 'Big Society': email protest presses AHRC to drop Tory mantra, *The Times Higher Education*, 7 April.

Karran, T. (2007). Academic freedom in Europe: a preliminary comparative analysis, *Higher Education Policy*, 20, 289–313.

——(2009). Academic freedom: in justification of a universal ideal, *Studies in Higher Education*, 34, 3, 263–283.

Kavanagh, D. (2000). Introduction. In I. Dale (Ed.) *Labour Party General Election Manifestos, 1900–1997* (pp. 1–8). London: Routledge.

Kennedy, B.D. (1997). *Academic Duty*. Cambridge, MA: Harvard University Press.

Kerr, C. (2001). *The Uses of the University*. 5th Edition, Cambridge, MA: Harvard University Press.

——(2008). The uses of the university, 1964. In W. Smith and T. Bender (Eds.) *American Higher Education Transformed 1940–2005: Documenting the National Discourse* (pp. 49–51). Baltimore, MD: The Johns Hopkins University Press.

Kim, T. (2010). Transnational academic mobility, knowledge and identity capital, *Discourse: Studies in the Cultural Politics of Education*, 31, 5, 577–591.

Kimball, R. (1990). *Tenured Radicals: How Politics Has Corrupted Our Higher Education*. Chicago: Ivan R. Dee.

King's College London (2011) *Profile 2011*. London: King's College.

Kirkland, J. (2008). University research management: an emerging profession in the developing world, *Technology Analysis and Strategic Management*, 20, 6, 717–726.

Klein, N. (2000). *No Logo*. London: Flamingo.

Klosaker, A. (2008) Academic professionalism in the managerialist era: a study of English universities, *Studies in Higher Education*, 33, 5, 513–525.

Knight, P. and Trowler, P. (2001). *Departmental Leadership in Higher Education*. Buckingham: Society for Research into Higher Education and the Open University Press.

Kogan, M., Moses, I. and El-Khawas, E. (1994). *Staffing in Higher Education*. London: Jessica Kingsley.

Kolsaker, A. (2008). Academic professionalism in the managerialist era: a study of English universities, *Studies in Higher Education*, 33, 5, 513–525.

Kouzes, J. and Posner, B. (1993). *Credibility: How Leaders Gain and Lose It, Why People Demand It*. San Francisco: Jossey-Bass.

Kuhn, T. (1962). *The Structure of Scientific Revolutions*. Chicago: University of Chicago Press.

Kwa, B.T. (1993). Righteous rights, *Far East Economic Review*, 17 June.

Lea, J. (2009). *Political Correctness and Higher Education: British and American Perspectives*. New York: Routledge.

Locke, W. (2007). *The Changing Academic Profession in the UK: Setting the Scene*. London: Universities UK.

Macfarlane, B. (2007). *The Academic Citizen: The Virtue of Service in University Life*. New York: Routledge.

——(2009). *Researching with Integrity: The Ethics of Academic Enquiry*. London: Routledge.

——(2011a). Professors as intellectual leaders: formation, identity and role, *Studies in Higher Education*, 36, 1, 57–73.

——(2011b). The morphing of academic practice: unbundling and the para-academic, *Higher Education Quarterly*, 65, 1, 59–73.

——(2011c). Teaching, integrity and the development of professional responsibility: why we need pedagogical phronesis. In C. Sugrue and T.D. Solbrekke (Eds.)

Professional Responsibility: New Horizons of Praxis? (pp. 72–86). Oxford University Press, Oxford.

Malcolm, W. and Tarling, N. (2007). *Crisis of Identity? The Mission and Management of Universities in New Zealand.* Wellington: Dunmore.

Martinson, B.C., Anderson, M.S. and De Vries, R.G. (2005). Scientists behaving badly, *Nature*, 435, 737–738.

Marturano, A. and Gosling, J. (2008). *Leadership: The Key Concepts.* London: Routledge.

Marquand, D. (2004). *The Decline of the Public: The Hollowing-Out of Citizenship.* Cambridge: Polity Press.

Mathias, H. (1991). The role of the university Head of Department, *Journal of Further and Higher Education*, 15, 3, 65–75.

Maxwell, N. (2009). From knowledge to wisdom: the need for an academic revolution. In R. Barnett and N. Maxwell (Eds.) *Wisdom in the University* (pp. 1–19). London: Routledge.

McGee Banks, C.A. (1995). Intellectual leadership and the influence of early African American scholars on multicultural education, *Educational Policy*, 9, 3, 260–280.

Mead, R. (2010). Learning by degrees, *The New Yorker*, 7 June, 21–22.

Merton, R.K. (1942). The normative structure of science. In N. Storer (Ed.) *The Sociology of Science: Theoretical and Empirical Investigations* (pp. 267–278). Chicago: The University of Chicago Press.

——(1947). Patterns of influence: local and cosmopolitan influentials. In R.K. Merton (Ed.) *Social Theory and Social Structure* (pp. 387–420). Glencoe, IL: The Free Press.

——(1948). The self-fulfilling prophesy, *The Antioch Review*, 8, 2, 193–210.

Metzger, W.P. (1988). Profession and constitution: two definitions of academic freedom in America, *Texas Law Review*, 1265–1322.

Middlehurst, R. (2008). Not enough science or not enough learning? Exploring the gaps between leadership theory and practice, *Higher Education Quarterly*, 62, 4, 322–339.

Mikes, G. (1946). *How to Be an Alien.* Harmondsworth: Penguin.

Moodie, G. (1986). The disintegrating chair: professors in Britain today, *European Journal of Education*, 21, 1, 43–56.

NCUP (National Conference of University Professors) (1991). *The Role of the Professoriate*, http://www.reading.ac.uk/ncup/poldocs/doc2.htm (accessed 13 March 2011).

Nelson, C. (2010). *No University is an Island: Saving Academic Freedom.* New York: New York University Press.

Nixon, J. (2010a). *Higher Education and the Public Good: Imagining the University.* London: Continuum.

——(2010b). Towards an ethics of academic practice: recognition, hospitality, and 'rooted cosmopolitanism'. *Hope Forum for Professional Ethics Lecture Series*, http://www.hope.ac.uk/education-news/hfpe-lecture.html (accessed 2 June 2011).

Nolan, M.P. (1997). *Standards in Public Life: First Report on Standards in Public Life.* London: HMSO.

Osinbajo, Y. and Ajayi, O. (1994) Human rights and economic development in developing countries, *The International Lawyer*, 28, 3, 727–742.

Parker, J. (2008). Comparing research and teaching in university promotion criteria, *Higher Education Quarterly*, 62, 3, 237–251.

Piercy, N.F. (1999). In search of excellence among business school professors: cowboys, chameleons, question-marks and quislings, *European Journal of Marketing*, 33, 7/8, 698–706.

Prospect (2005). Global public intellectuals poll, *Prospect Magazine*, November, 116.

——(2008). The 2008 top 100 intellectuals poll, June, *Prospect Magazine*, xxx.

Rayner, S., Fuller, M., McEwen, L. and Roberts, H. (2010). Managing leadership in the UK university: a case for researching the missing professoriate, *Studies in Higher Education*, 35, 6, 617–631.

Reisz, M. (2008). Caroline Thomas, 1959–2008, *Times Higher Education*, 6 November, 23.

——(2009a). Michael Majerus, 1954–2009, *Times Higher Education*, 26 February, 21.

——(2009b). Ken Green, 1946–2009, *Times Higher Education*, 12 March, 27.

——(2009c). John Golby, 1935–2009, *Times Higher Education*, 19 March, 27.

——(2009d). Roy Anthony Becher, 1930–2009, *Times Higher Education*, 2 April, 27.

——(2009e). Sir Neil MacCormick, 1941–2009, *Times Higher Education*, 7 May, 23.

——(2009f). Tyrrell Burgess, 1931–2009, *Times Higher Education*, 14 May, 23.

——(2009g). Olivia Harris, 1948–2009, *Times Higher Education*, 21 May, 23.

——(2009h). Sir Clive Granger, 1934–2009, *Times Higher Education*, 18 June, 23.

——(2009i). Peter Townsend, 1928–2009, *Times Higher Education*, June 25, 23.

——(2009j). Sheila Rodwell, 1947–2009, *Times Higher Education*, 13 August, 23.

——(2009k). Chris Lamb, 1950–2009, *Times Higher Education*, 17 September, 23.

——(2009l). Ellie Scrivens, 1954–2008, *Times Higher Education*, 27 November, 23.

——(2010a). Sir James Black, 1924–2010, *Times Higher Education*, 22 April, 23.

——(2010b). Fred Halliday, 1946–2010, *Times Higher Education*, 6 May, 21.

Rhode, D.L. (2001). The professional responsibilities of professors, *Journal of Legal Education*, 51, 2, 158–166.

Roberts, P. (2007). Intellectuals, tertiary education and questions of difference, *Educational Philosophy and Theory*, 39, 5, 480–493.

Rooney, D. and McKenna, B. (2009). Knowledge, wisdom and intellectual leadership: a question of the future and knowledge-based sustainability, *International Journal of Learning and Intellectual Capital*, 6, 1/2, 52–70.

Ross, A. (2011). Rights, freedom and offshore academics, *University World News*, 1 May, http://www.universityworldnews.com/article.php?story=20110429165843773 (accessed 2 May 2011).

Russell, C. (1993). *Academic Freedom*. London: Routledge.

Said, E. (1985). *Orientalism*. London: Penguin.

——(1994). *Representations of the Intellectual*. London: Vintage Books.

Shattock, M. (2003). *Managing Successful Universities*. Buckingham: Society for Research into Higher Education and the Open University Press.

Shils, E. (1997). *The Calling of Education: The Academic Ethic and Other Essays on Higher Education*. Chicago: University of Chicago Press.

Siegelman, S.S. (1991). Assassins and zealots: variations in peer review, *Radiology*, 178, 3, 636–642.

Sikes, P. (2006). Working in a new university: in the shadow of the RAE?, *Studies in Higher Education*, 31, 5, 555–568.

Simon Fraser University (2010). *SFU Strategic Plan 2010–2015*, www.sfu.ca/vpresearch/docs/SRP2010_15.pdf (accessed 15 December 2010).

Slaughter, S. and Lesley, L. (1997). *Academic Capitalism: Politics, Policies and the Entrepreneurial University.* Baltimore, MD: The Johns Hopkins University Press.

Slaughter, S. and Rhoades, G. (2004). *Academic Capitalism and the New Economy: Markets, States, and Higher Education.* Baltimore, MD: The Johns Hopkins University Press.

Smith, D. (2008). Academics or executives? Continuity and change in the roles of pro-vice-chancellors, *Higher Education Quarterly,* 62, 4, 340–357.

Sotirakou, T. (2004). Coping with conflict within the entrepreneurial university: threat or challenge for Heads of Department in the UK higher education context, *International Review of Administrative Sciences,* 70, 2, 345–372.

Startup, R. (1976). The role of the Departmental Head, *Studies in Higher Education,* 1, 2, 233–243.

Stogdill, R.M. (1974). *Handbook of Leadership.* New York: Free Press.

Strike, T. (2010). Evolving academic career pathways in England. In G. Gordon and C. Whitchurch (Eds.) *Academic and Professional Identities in Higher Education: The Challenges of a Diversifying Workforce* (pp. 77–97). New York: Routledge.

Taylor, J., Hallstron, I., Salanterä, S. and Begley, C. (2009) How to be a professor: what the books don't tell you, *Nurse Education Today,* 29, 7, 691–693.

Thody, A. (2011). Emeritus professors of an English university: how is the wisdom of the aged used?, *Studies in Higher Education,* 36, 6, 637–653.

Thorens, J. (2006). Liberties, freedom and autonomy: a few reflections on academia's estate, *Higher Education Policy,* 19, 87–110.

Tight, M. (2002). What does it mean to be a professor?, *Higher Education Review,* 34, 15–31.

Townsend, P. (1979). *Poverty in the United Kingdom,* Harmondsworth: Penguin.

Travis, J. (2009). Academic charged with insulting the monarchy, *University World News,* 1 February, 61, http://www.universityworldnews.com/article.php?story=20090130101017692 (accessed 3 February 2011).

Trow, M. (2010a). Comparative reflections on leadership in higher education. In M. Burrage (Ed.) *Martin Trow. Twentieth Century Education: Elite to Mass to Universal* (pp. 435–61). Baltimore, MD: The Johns Hopkins University Press.

——(2010b). Managerialism and the academic profession. In M. Burrage (Ed.) *Martin Trow. Twentieth Century Education: Elite to Mass to Universal* (pp. 271–298). Baltimore, MD: The Johns Hopkins University Press.

——(2010c). Leadership and organization: the case of biology at Berkeley. In M. Burrage (Ed.) *Martin Trow. Twentieth Century Education: Elite to Mass to Universal* (pp. 397–432). Baltimore, MD: The Johns Hopkins University Press.

University College London (2011). *UCL Grand Challenges,* http://www.ucl.ac.uk/research/grand-challenges (accessed 25 May 2010).

University of Auckland (2011). *Strategic Research Initiatives,* http://www.auckland.ac.nz/uoa/home/about/research/strategic-research-initiatives (accessed 8 January 2011).

University of Hong Kong (2011). *Strategic Research Areas and Themes,* http://www.hku.hk/research/sras/ (accessed 3 January 2011).

University of Stellenbosch (2011). *Research Initiatives,* http://www0.sun.ac.za/research/en/strategic-research-themes-srts (accessed 14 January 2011).

University of Sussex (2008). *Criteria for the Appointment and Promotion of Academic Faculty,* http://www.sussex.ac.uk/Units/staffing/personnl/reviews/academic/criteria.doc (accessed 17 July 2009).

Universities UK (2008). *The Changing Academic Profession in the UK and Beyond*, www.universitiesuk.ac.uk/.../The%20Changing%20HE%20Profession.pdf (accessed 5 February 2011).

Van Hooft, S. (2009). Dialogue, virtue and ethics. In J. Strain, R. Barnett and P. Jarvis (Eds.) *Universities, Ethics and Professions* (pp. 81–93). New York: Routledge.

Vogel, M.P. (2009). The professionalism of professors at German Fachhochschulen, *Studies in Higher Education*, 34, 8, 873–888.

Waitere, H.J., Wright, J., Tremaine, M., Brown, S. and Pausé, C.J. (2011). Choosing whether to resist or reinforce the new managerialism: the impact of performance-based research funding on academic identity, *Higher Education Research and Development*, 30, 2, 205–217.

Warner, D. and Palfreyman, D. (2000). *Higher Education Management: The Key Elements*. 2nd edition. Buckingham: Society for Research into Higher Education/ Open University Press.

Watson, D. (2007). *Managing Civic and Community Engagement*. Maidenhead: McGraw-Hill/Open University Press.

——(2009). *The Question of Morale: Managing Happiness and Unhappiness in University Life*. Maidenhead: Open University Press.

Wepner, S.B., D'Onofrio, A. and Wilhite, S.C. (2008). The leadership dimensions of education deans, *Journal of Teacher Education*, 59, 2, 153–169.

Whitburn, J., Mealing, M., and Cox, C. (1976). *People in Polytechnics*. Surrey: Society for Research into Higher Education.

Whitchurch, C. (2006). *Professional Managers in UK Higher Education: Preparing for Complex Futures*. London: LfHE.

Whitchurch, C. and Gordon, G. (2010). Diversifying academic and professional identities in higher education: some management challenges, *Tertiary Education and Management*, 16, 2, 129–144.

Wildavsky, B. (2010). *The Great Brain Race: How Global Universities are Reshaping the World*. Princeton, NJ: Princeton University Press.

Wilson, L. (1942). *The Academic Man*. New York: Oxford University Press.

——(1979). *American Academics: Then and Now*. New York: Oxford University Press.

Winter, R. (2009). Academic manager or managed academic? Academic identity schisms in higher education, *Journal of Higher Education Policy and Management*, 31, 2, 121–131.

Wright Mills, C. (1959). *The Sociological Imagination*. Oxford: Oxford University Press.

——(1963). The social role of the intellectual. In I.L. Horowitz (Ed.) *Power, Politics and People: The Collected Essays of C. Wright Mills* (pp. 292–304). New York: Oxford University Press.

Yuchen, Z. (2007). The Pan Zhichang incident, *Chinese Education and Society*, 40, 6, 20–30.

Yukl, G. (2002). *Leadership in Organisations*. Upper Saddle River, NJ: Prentice Hall.

Index